Moon City Review
2013

Moon City Review is a publication of Moon City Press at Missouri State University and is distributed by the University of Arkansas Press. Exchange subscriptions with literary magazines are encouraged. The editors of *Moon City Review* contract First North American Serial Rights, all rights reverting to the writers upon publication. The views expressed by authors in *Moon City Review* do not necessarily reflect the opinions of its editors, Moon City Press, or Missouri State University.

All other correspondence should be sent to the appropriate editor, using the following information:

Moon City Review
Department of English
Missouri State University
901 South National Avenue
Springfield, MO 65897

Submissions are considered at http://mooncitypress.com/mcr/. For more information, please consult www.mooncitypress.com.

ISBN: 978-0-913785-44-7

Moon City Review 2013

moon city press
springfield missouri

Parking Lot by Sarah Williams, oil on board, 12" by 12", 2012.

Sherman by Sarah Williams, oil on board, 24" by 24", 2012.

Table of Contents

Poetry

Fiction

Nonfiction

Art

Translations

Staff

Editor
Michael Czyzniejewski

Poetry Editor
Lanette Cadle

Nonfiction Editor
John Turner

Fiction Editor
Jennifer Murvin

Reviews Editor
Michael Czyzniejewski

Managing Editor
Angelia Northrup-Rivera

Assistant Editors
Jessica Boykin
Anthony Isaac Bradley
Derek Cowsert
Matt Kimberlin
Lora Knight
Timothy Leyrson
Joseph Lucido
Andrew Myers
Jeff Van Booven
Satarah Wheeler

Advisory Editors
James Baumlin
W.D. Blackmon
Sara Burge
Marcus Cafagña
Jane Hoogestraat
Richard Neumann

Special Thanks
Karen Craigo
Toshiya Kamei

Jeff Gundy

Waterfall

So I didn't get the instructions. So the pond's full
of grainy duckweed, bumblebees in damp clover,

dragonflies and damselflies, twittery birds. Young Will
keeps saying things like, "This could be lava!" Two hawks

swoop and soar. I think they might see paradise
just over the brow of the hill, and because I'm not

Kafka if I could climb those skies myself the mighty
keeper at the gate would usher me in graciously, show me

to the holy sunporch where God and I would sit, drink
coffee and compare our griefs, our big defeats and

little victories. And the sweet air will zephyr all around us,
carrying birdsong and creek babble, and we will agree

that things are dismal but not unusual, and that a certain
cockeyed hope is still required of us. We'll walk a long way

through the beeches and tulip poplars, and at the waterfall
we will peel our clothes and splash in the shallows,

as close as we dare to the roar and rush, and its every
syllable will come clear suddenly. And then everyone

will be there, your friends and mine, our enemies, too,
all the strangers holy and unholy, and in the water's spell

we will touch our perfect bodies and our minds and
remember everything. And we will laugh and dance

and make meta- and physical love until the very universe
shivers and glows. And when at last we are healed, sated,

complete, we will lie down in the long meadow grass,
the dragonflies basking and soaring all around, and sleep

in the roar and the silence for as long as our dreams require.

Chad Davidson

Casual Labor

Not painting the wall but painting *at* it,
taking drags from a cigarette, your hand
speckled with some ludicrous latex like
White-Hot Felt, Tumbleweed Shadow.
Or cutting half the lawn, the ragged fringes
left to the cat, who's nothing if not casual
in his labor, notionally hunting a cat's-eye
marble among the dust mites. But what the hell.
It's summer in Georgia, a state that, for all we know,
invented the term, the idea, of *casual labor,*
which sounds so much better than *part-time,*
more immune to the offering of benefits,
which is yet another evasion, the lexical equivalent
of fake sugars with their own gingerbread
names—*Splenda, Truvia, Sweet'N Low*—names
simultaneously casual and laborious, which provide
the promise of zero-calorie desires, weightless
as the language through which they are broadcast,
which, to you, looking on your average lawn
from your semi-exquisite room, casts a shadow
over the cat and its dream of limbless mice,
a shadow that, if you weren't casually at labor
in the betterment of space, rendering that much
more soothing your interior, you might just call
Remarkable or *Splendid* or *White Hot Splenda.*

Trista Edwards

The Light Bulb People

They watch us from the convex
belly of incandescence.

Like babies, they slide and inch
up the cords, breaching glass

and invention, that they may inspect
and know what twists the world.

In their handheld universe, they only
tilt their heads and ponder

the curiosities of unfurling teeth.
Innocent as fingers they corset us

in light as we unknowingly perform
the odd little number for their swollen blinks,

hot and pink for the clapping.
Do they listen too? Our soft and watery

speak? Grappling at the corners
of our mumbles? Do they avail

the rotting fruit, the flies that quicken
to the bin, filching every minute

we think we are alone? Thieving
little angels, swinging on a current.

Matt Cashion

Awful Pretty

Just after midnight, for the third straight night, Ma calls and wakes me from my shallow sleep to say she's hearing a strange voice coming from the woods behind her house again, louder this time, and she is scared. I've been telling her it's just an animal, maybe a heartbroken skunk who has lost its mate, but she is past the point of listening.

"Come listen, Benny," she says. "Someone is singing out there. I'm not crazy. I can hear perfectly well."

"It's just an animal, Ma." I keep my eyes closed. I yawn. I've been sleep-deprived for a long time myself, for my own good reasons.

"I can't hear you, honey. Take off your mask." I remove the sleeping mask connected to the oxygen tank Dr. Peikart prescribed for the apnea Dr. Lupi diagnosed three months ago after Dr. Adamczyk watched a video of me sleeping, which showed I had stopped breathing seventeen times within six hours.

"If we don't get some sleep soon," Ma says, "we'll die from insomnia."

The we includes Oscar, her goldfish, who is sensitive to stress. When Ma can't sleep, Oscar gets nervous and swims in manic circles.

"Then the blood will be on your hands, Benny. How would you like to live with yourself after that, honey?"

My alarm is set for six a.m. because I have to work for the eleventh straight day. And I'm already feeling the early stages of what is likely a lung infection caught from one of the hundred-plus sickees I admitted to the emergency room during today's twelve-hour shift. If I remain sleep-deprived, my immunities will collapse and this sickness will blossom into a full-blown condition that will render me lifeless for seven to ten days, during which time I'll be tempted to swallow the bottle of Temazepam I keep on my bedside table for such occasions, which I came close to doing three months ago, when I was in bed for *thirteen* straight days.

"Come listen, Benny. Your sister's not answering her phone. I called her first, of course. God knows where she's running the streets. Bring your gun."

"I don't have a gun, Ma."

"What kind of man don't have a gun these days? I'm asking for your help, Benny. I haven't been myself since that thing next door. You know that."

I yawn. *That thing next door* happened two months ago when this pretty normal-seeming guy, Wayne Houston, decapitated his seven-year-old disabled son. It made national news. He put his son's decapitated head in his wheelchair and parked the wheelchair at the end of the driveway so the boy's mother could see it when she came home. *The Daily Sun* said that Wayne said, "I wanted his mother to see what she had done. I wanted her to feel stupid."

"I think it's a gospel song," Ma says. "It's awful spooky."

I take my broom handle and my flashlight. I broke my broom last week while I was murdering a spider in the bathroom. The flashlight, I keep on my bedside table for late-night bathroom trips. I haven't replaced my nightlight and the spiders keep multiplying, probably from the neighbors' dirty apartments. My best friend, Bruce, who works with me in triage, is married to a woman who lost her foot from a brown recluse bite. They met in a bar, actually, where she used her missing foot as a conversation piece. Bruce promised to cure her phantom pain, and I guess he did, because I attended their wedding fifteen years ago. It was the last joyful thing I witnessed. After that, my father, Dr. Benjamin Bent, Sr., a surgeon, killed himself over a botched operation. A week later, my wife moved to Tokyo with Dr. Maleszewski, taking my autistic daughter, Kimberly, then three years old. My wife claimed I would forever be a hopeless mama's boy. She claimed I was too self-centered to help my own troubled sister, who constantly left whiny messages. She claimed I was in love with Bruce. I denied nothing. I didn't fight for custody. I looked forward to being alone, but when I was alone, I stopped sleeping. I blame the loud neighbors and their loud arguments, which get louder after I bang the walls. And lately, I've had dizzy spells, which Dr. Demaerschalk said she'd like to keep an eye on. Then Dr. Demaerschalk had a stroke. She left her patients unattended and offered no referrals, which I found both inconvenient and unprofessional.

When my wife left, I moved into an apartment complex a half-mile from Ma's house. In the past year, some new neighbors (I suspect the shirtless, tattooed Hispanic kids who like to flaunt their underwear) have committed inexplicable acts of cruelty towards me, such as plastering hateful bumper stickers to my car. Last month, it was this one: "Silly faggot, dicks are for chicks." I plastered a "People Suck" sticker over it and continue to ignore them.

And now, just after midnight, as I stumble toward my car, I find a dead cat on the driver's side windshield—the wild black cat I'd been leaving milk for. A line of blood, still wet, had spilled from one nostril. I stare at its whiskers and its open eyes, its soft paws and its bloody nose, and I bend to vomit. This is what it's come to. I go back to my apartment for a bag, put the kitty in it, tie the bag, then drop it in the Dumpster so her body won't be mutilated by wild animals. On the way to Ma's, I plot ways to mutilate the kids who did this.

Behind Ma's house, I crunch dead leaves and stand between her open bedroom window and the woods, wishing I'd worn a coat over the robe I put over my pajamas. I shine my light into the woods and listen. I don't hear anything.

"Do you hear anything?" Ma yells through her window.

A man says, "Now you've scared it off."

I shine my light at her window. "Is someone in there with you?"

The man says, "Is that him? He took long enough."

"Who's in there?"

"Did you hear the singing?" Ma says. "It sounded like a tormented angel."

I walk to her window. She is seventy, still in better shape than most everyone I know, from the neck down, at least. She gets a little scared at night while she watches her crime shows, but I don't blame her, especially after what happened next door.

When I press my nose to the screen, Bengay smacks me at once, along with menthol, mothballs, and some old familiar gloom that knocks me back forty years.

She says, "I can hear you breathing, honey. Is your asthma acting up?"

"He's too fat," the man says. "He was born too fat."

I raise the flashlight, cup my other hand around my left eye and see—sitting on the far edge of the bed with his back facing me, wearing the tank-top preferred by older men—an older man.

Ma says, "Turn off that light. You're scaring Oscar."

The man turns his profile toward me.

"Who's that man sitting on your bed?" I say.

"You know Dr. Wright. He delivered you into this world forty-five years ago."

"Hiya, Benjamin. How's things on the first floor?"

"What're you doing in there?"

"I was inspecting your mother's rash, likely caused by an ingrown pubic hair that got infected. I applied some ointment, but we'll have to keep monitoring the situation."

"Did you hear it, Benny? That singing? Do you think I'm crazy, now, Mr. Big Shot Triage Man? Wasn't it awful pretty?"

I hold on to the side of the house. I say, "We'll have to keep monitoring the situation."

"Listen to you," she says. "You sound just like a doctor."

"I have to go now."

"Goodnight, honey," Ma says.

"Good night, *honey*," Dr. Wright says.

I try to sleep. Even a nightmare would be nice, to get my mind off Dr. Wright's house call, and for a couple of seconds I dream of swimming in manic circles, but the rest is a black-and-white blur. Dr. Thorsteinsdottir, the therapist on the fourth floor I see every Tuesday during my lunch hour, says depressed people don't remember their dreams as often as happy people, which depresses me. I'd be happy if I could remember any small part of just one dream.

The next morning, on my way to the hospital, after sleeping two hours, I stop at Ma's like I do every morning. For breakfast. She usually cooks me four strips of bacon and three eggs fried in bacon grease, a bowl of grits with extra salt and extra butter, toast with raspberry jelly and honey, coffee, and a glass of pineapple juice with a splash of water.

Ma's street, Magnolia Lane, is a cul-de-sac shaped like a hook. All the magnolia trees were removed because of a fungus, but Ma had hers cut *before* they got sick. To be safe, she said, before they crushed her and Oscar in their sleep, even though the trees were only house-high and not big enough to hurt anything. At the beginning of the street is a nursing home I thought would be nice for Ma one day, but it's under investigation because two residents, roommates, were caught making and distributing crystal meth. Across from the nursing home is an old church that a preacher turned into a "pain management clinic," recently shut down for selling pills to middle-schoolers. The road is lined with ranch homes built in the 1960s, big yards and deep woods forty miles south of Nashville in this town where my parents were born, and where I have spent my life, loving it and hating it, imagining other places, going nowhere.

When I pull up, Ma is sitting at the end of her driveway, in her bathrobe, reading *The Daily Sun*. There are leaves all around her, and the wind is blowing her thin hair, but she seems perfectly content sitting there in the near-darkness reading her newspaper.

"What're you doing?" I say.

"Reading the obituaries to see if your sister's in here."

I look around the neighborhood to see if anyone is watching, but it's too early, and all the nice neighbors I knew as a child are dead or gone anyway.

"I had a dizzy spell," she says. "I bent for the paper and fell right over."

Wayne Houston's house is still for sale. On the night he cut off his son's head, I stayed with Ma because she got scared with all the cop cars and media trucks and all the yellow tape. Once, from Ma's window, I saw two cops step from Wayne's house with their hands over their eyes, sobbing from what they'd seen in there. All I knew about Wayne was that he'd come from Michigan to work at the GM plant. He told me this when he brought over a mac-and-cheese casserole after Dad died, which he said he'd made himself. After that, we only waved a few times and never had a real conversation, even after the GM plant closed last year, which I feel bad about—not talking to him. I guess his wife moved back to Michigan.

"So I decided to stay here and read the paper until someone showed up."

Across the street, a skeleton has fallen on its face, half-buried in wet leaves. The yard next to it holds a deflated ghost. Both porches hold rotting jack-o'-lanterns.

Just then, Dr. Wright comes up behind me carrying a walking stick shaped like a scythe.

"A woman was raped in the Target parking lot," Ma says. "I never have liked Target."

"I'll tell you who has the best-looking place on the street," Dr. Wright says. "It's that black family down at the end who moved in last month. They keep a good-looking place."

"That's an offensive—last month?" I wonder how long Dr. Wright has been making house calls.

"Would anyone like to help me up?" Ma says.

"It was the last of September," Wright says. "Just after I married your mother."

"I've read every obituary twice. I don't see your sister. I wonder what picture she'd want to use, anyway. She always hated getting her picture made. Never once smiled that I remember."

"Are you having chest pains?" Dr. Wright says.

"No, but my ass is numb."

"I'm referring to Benjamin. He looks a little woozy and he's holding his heart."

It's true. I'm woozy and I'm holding my heart. I don't know how I missed Dr. Wright having married my mother. Maybe he goes for long walks every morning while I eat breakfast. Maybe he sleeps late. Or leaves early. Dr. Thorsteinsdottir says depressed people often lose their powers of observation. She says if I noticed how miserable others are, I'd feel better. She says I should ask others about their suffering. Mostly, she says, I should start asking myself better questions about myself, but I'm not sure where to start.

"Let's get you inside," Dr. Wright says.

"I'm ready," Ma says.

He grabs my elbow and guides me slowly up the driveway, using his walking stick, telling me *nice and easy now, everything's going to be fine.*

Behind us, Ma says, "Another baby was found in the Duck River inside a garbage bag. Third one this year."

Dr. Wright sits me at the kitchen table, brings me a paper bag and tells me to breathe into it while he goes back for Ma. I want to go to work and tell Bruce what's going on. But it's Monday, so he'll only want to talk about how he spent the weekend helping his differently-abled wife meet the new challenges she set for herself, which I already heard all about on Friday: hikes, karate lessons, kickball games, a waltz, etc.

Then I think of calling my daughter, Kimberly, in Tokyo. She is eighteen now. Just so she'll remember me, her father. Maybe she would say, "I love you." The last time I talked to her, many months ago, she said she was afraid to touch the same phone her stepfather, Dr. Maleszewski, touched. I invited her then to come live with me, but she said my sighs hurt her ears, and Ma's house hurt her nose, and the town hurt her eyes, and the only place where she felt safe was in her own bedroom closet, which she had trouble leaving, which is my fault. I'm afraid she inherited my genes for being strange and large and lonely. I would visit her, but I'm afraid of flying. I've never been on a plane. No way could I remain in the air all the way to Tokyo. I'd like to hear her voice now, but the time difference makes it too early there anyway, a mistake I've made before, which Kimberly scolded me for by saying, "You forgot the time difference, Daddy-doofus. Now you've woken up *my parents*." Doofus was one of her first words, learned from her mother. A year later, she put Daddy in front of Doofus, and continues to do so, insisting it's an endearment.

Dr. Wright comes in with Ma, both of them giggling.

She says, "You want some breakfast, Benny?"

I answer.

"Move that bag away from your mouth, honey."

"Yes ma'am, please."

"You know what Anthony eats for breakfast? Bran cereal with a prune. Then he poops at six a.m. like clockwork."

"And now," he says, "I'm off to the Y for my 1K swim, 3K run, and 5K bike ride. I'm behind schedule after being up so late. The globe is cockeyed off its axis. But I'll be on the battlefield by two."

"Isn't he amazing?" Ma says. "After all that exercise, he does his servicework. He walks around Franklin and talks to dead soldiers."

"*They* talk to *me*, dear. They cry, and I console. All six thousand, two hundred and fifty-two of them." He kisses Ma on the lips, pats my head and literally whistles "Dixie" on his way out the door.

"Isn't he cute?" Ma says. "The last of a dying breed, that man. So chivalrous." Then she whistles the same tune while measuring her grits.

"Why wasn't I informed of your marriage?"

"It wasn't a secret, Benny."

"But why did you have to marry him?"

11

"On our first date he listened to my heart and said my arthritis was verging on critical, so he recommended he move in. I said we'd have to get married first under the eyes of God, then he put a handkerchief on the ground and proposed on bended knee. It's nice to have a man around the house. Isn't he handsome? And such bedside manner. Such a soft touch."

"Could I have some bourbon?"

She squeezes the orange bulb of a medicine dropper over my coffee until a drop of bourbon comes out. She does the same for hers. This is what Dad had done for both of them every morning of their married lives for forty years until the day he went to work and removed a patient's leg instead of her appendix. Later, after the patient complained of the missing leg *and* the persisting appendix pain, Dad carried a lethal dose of sodium pentothal to his Cadillac, which he'd mistakenly parked in the reserved space of the CEO, Mr. Bathanti, and injected himself.

When I get to my desk, I see Bruce has called in sick. I call him immediately to tell him about my night and my morning. His wife picks up and says, "Listen. You call my husband again and I'll march very quickly to wherever you are and personally stomp your fat ass until you bleed to death, is that clear?" She hangs up before I can answer. I wonder what Bruce has told her. The truth? That he'd rather be with me, except he'd feel guilty leaving a one-footed woman? The fluorescent lights spin around my eyes while a distant phone rings. Then a man runs in screaming, covered in burns after setting a bee-hive on fire, which he did for revenge, he tells me, after suffering a sting. Then a boy comes in staring at a small computer he's carrying, earplugs in, a thin nail stuck between his eyes which his mother says his father put there with a nailgun from across the room (which means extra paperwork for me), then a failed overdoser, then a baby with a blood-soaked diaper, then an Amish kid by ambulance—maybe a broken neck after a truck driver creamed his horse (dead) and buggy (totaled) on the Columbia Pike, plus a broken foot caused by the EMT who slammed the ambulance doors too quickly—then the guy in the chicken suit who waves outside Fred's Chicken Palace limps in carrying his chicken head, the feathers around his right thigh bloody from a passing gunshot, then a priest with chest pains confesses to me that he has done unspeakable things and asks me to hold his hand while I call another priest he knows (long distance) who administers last rites too loudly over the phone's intercom, then Dr. Thorsteinsdottir, my own counselor from the fourth floor, suffers a seizure while listening to a patient and gets admitted at once, nonresponsive, which means I'll miss tomorrow's appointment. And between all these cases is the normal and constant onslaught of the sick and flu-ridden and fevered battalion of doubled-over people who vomit into disposable cups and cough into my face while I ask them to repeat the spellings of their names and their home addresses and verify their insurance (no one ever asks how I'm doing) until, at 9 p.m., I go home and fall into bed, feeling sick myself, too tired to eat anything but the box of cherry-filled chocolate-topped Krispy Kremes I pick up on the way home, which puts me right to sleep.

Ma calls at midnight.

"It's louder tonight, Benny—that awful-pretty, terrible-sad singing. Come listen."

I ask her why Dr. Wright, her "man around the house," can't take care of it.

"Take off your mask, honey."

I remove my mask and repeat my question.

"He won't wake up, Benny. You should look at him, too, while you're here. I'm scared. And your sister's still not answering her phone. We're very upset."

I'm pretty sure I have a fever. But I get up anyway, grab my broom handle and flashlight, put a coat on over the robe I put on over my pajamas, find my slippers and slip them on. When I get to my car, I see that all four of my tires are missing. My car (Dad's old Cadillac) is up on blocks, and the wheels are gone. I'm sure, at this moment, if the entire gang of hoodlums stepped forward, I would use my broomstick to bludgeon them to death. But no one is around. All the lights in all the apartments are out. So I walk. I walk through the field between the complex and the car wash, through the center stall, then go uphill behind the nursing home to get to Magnolia Lane, certain my fever is nearing 102.

The door key Ma gave me doesn't fit. I knock and ring the bell and knock and ring the bell and knock.

"Who is it?" Ma says.

"It's me, Ma. Why did you change the locks?"

"Is that you, Benny?"

"It's me, Ma."

She lets me in. She says, "Anthony changed the locks to keep out the enemy. He's in the bedroom. Did you bring your stethoscope?"

I find Dr. Wright lying completely naked, open eyes pointed toward the ceiling. His erect penis also points toward the ceiling. Ma stands behind me, leaning her head on my back. Through her bedroom window, I hear, for the first time, a strange and beautiful voice singing something in a foreign language.

"Did I kill him, Benny? He said he'd taken an extra vitamin, then he applied some ointment to his plunger and asked me to sit on top of him so he could apply it, and it felt pretty good, Benny, I'm not ashamed to tell you—so maybe I got carried away and killed him. And listen to that singing. I know you hear it."

"I hear it. I'll take a look."

"You should examine Anthony first, Benny. Anthony should have priority."

"I'll get to him as soon as I can," I say.

She starts crying. She says, "He'll be right back, Anthony. He has to see about the voice first, then he'll see you."

The voice is a loud single-note wail that might be some European word for "help." Or either it's not a word at all. I go through the back yard and step into the woods, duck beneath low limbs, step over fallen limbs, push through vines. I shine my light in front of me and stop once to knock away a spiderweb stretched between branches. A sweatball pops through my forehead—I'm in no shape for a hike—and I start breathing through my mouth. The air is cold enough to burn my lungs a little, but I continue toward the voice, which circles my head and retreats and comes back. I feel my way in a zig-zaggy pattern, holding my broomstick (which I can't even see) in front of my face.

The voice sounds like it's singing of terrible things it doesn't know the words for. I step over a limb and lose a slipper. This is a voice that has seen more blood than me. A dizzy spell hits me so hard I have to lean against a tree. The voice sounds like a child is crying at the same pitch that an old woman is wailing. I lift my bare foot. I picture faces on fire. The tree I'm leaning against is too thin. The voice is holding a note now that is being sustained longer than seems possible for any human. I lower my bare foot to the cold ground. I picture the voice bubbling up from some primitive pool of lava a few thousand miles below me. It's painful and playful and heartbreaking and honest and ancient and new, intended for no audience. The voice knocks something loose between my throat and chest. It swipes the dust off my eyes and squeezes my tear ducts. I hold steady to my tree, suddenly very weak, ready to sob like I haven't sobbed since—since I don't know when.

When I lift my light, I see an abandoned car nearly swallowed-up with weeds. The voice, very clearly, is coming from inside the car. It stops.

"Benny?"

I don't answer.

"You're breathing hard, Benny. Is your asthma acting up?"

I shine the light toward the back window and see my sister's face.

"What're you doing in there?" I say.

"What's it sound like? You should sit down before you have a heart attack."

It sounds like a good idea. I step through some high weeds, put my broomstick under my arm and tug on the driver's side door, which opens on my third pull. I fall behind the wheel, rest my bare foot on the gas pedal, close the door and exhale.

Penny says, "Turn off that light."

I do. I stare through the dark windshield. I say, "Your singing was—I can't believe that was you. So much better than any of your recitals."

"How would you know?"

She has a point. I never went to any of her recitals. In fact, I'm not sure, before tonight, that I've ever heard her sing. She's fifteen years younger—Ma calls her "my accident." She was three when I went to college, seven when I got married, fifteen when Dad killed himself. There are large sections of her life I know nothing about. I do know that everyone praised her singing while she grew up, promised her a brilliant future. She attended Belmont on a scholarship, dropped out when the teachers criticized her, transferred to a state school, changed majors, dropped out again, had a brief visit to a psychiatric ward, married a man she met in rehab, divorced, returned to rehab, lived with other men, lost jobs, lived on credit cards. Most of this, I learned from her voice messages.

She says, "Wayne used to bring me out here. Before he did what he did. We used to hang out in the back seat."

"Hang out?"

"Have sex, Benjamin. Get loaded and have sex. She cheated on him first, though, which is what no one knows. He wanted her to take their son back to Michigan so we could be together. He was such a good listener."

"Did he ever mention me?"

She sighs at this. I picture her eyes rolling. "Why would he mention you? He was a good listener, Benny. He was interested in *me*. But you think you know somebody, you know? I guess you can never really know anyone very well for sure, can you?"

There's something accusatory in her tone, but I don't respond. She starts humming. The humming is peaceful and melodic and more soulful than any humming I've ever heard.

"Dad's favorite," I say.

She stops.

I say, "Do you feel like singing it?"

On the first note to "Ave Maria," my hands fall from the wheel and I close my eyes and see a different shade of darkness that makes me dizzy with how light I feel inside of it. It's the same dizziness that hits me when I imagine Kimberly stepping straight from her Tokyo closet into my well-lit living room, smiling.

When she finishes, I open my eyes. I wipe my cheeks. I say, "Wow. That was really—I really, I don't know why I'm so—I'm not feeling too—."

"Did you know our mother lost her marbles and married Dr. Wright?"

I wipe my eyes again. I take a deep breath. "How did you know?"

"I've been living next door. Wayne gave me a key the night before he did what he did. His wife kept a well-stocked pantry, I'll give her that—lots of beans. Ma couldn't live in sin, of course, and I see Dr. Wright leave every morning before dawn, then I see you show up to stuff your face after that. I haven't slept in a very long time."

"I didn't know."

"You're not very observant."

I look through the windshield, then out the window. "It's peaceful out here."

"It's the only place that makes sense. I never want to be out there again around all those people who will be staring at me because I was involved with Wayne. Everyone knows we were sleeping together. I know they know. I can't go back out there."

"I can't either. I'm having a—."

"And now Ma's lost her mind and married Dr. Wright, who's crazy too. Don't you think Dr. Wright's crazy?"

"Yes, but he's dead. He's lying in Ma's bed right now, dead as a post."

"What?"

"Stiff as a board."

"What?"

"Dead as a dead cat."

She pauses. I picture her mouth hanging open. "Did you call anyone?"

I don't answer.

"Christ, Benny. You left Ma alone with Dr. Wright's dead body in her bed? Are you serious? What the fuck is wrong with you?"

I'm not sure how to answer this. I start humming. I hum "Ave Maria," but it sounds ugly, even to my ears.

"Do you ever ask yourself why your wife left you or why your daughter hates you? Do you ever ask yourself why you'll always be alone? You make my stomach hurt."

She reaches over the seat, grabs my flashlight, then takes off through the woods, straight toward Wayne's back door. It's just like her to steal my flashlight and leave me stranded.

There are no crickets, no tree frogs, no owls, no little feet scurrying, no wind to clang the leaves, no streetlights, no traffic noise, no crackling from a power line, no moon, not a single sound or light from the whole dead neighborhood. Penny's singing voice rises inside my head again and stays. It swirls around and swells. It pushes its feet against one ear and its hands against the other ear. It burrows, climbs, crawls, stomps, and whispers. It claws the back of one eye. It drops a jackhammer, apologizes, winks, glues a teacup, screams the color orange. It builds a house of dynamite on a cloud that sits on the ocean and asks sweetly, please, to be tucked in. Then pauses. Then mocks the sound of ticking. Then sings again, more loudly.

I grip the steering wheel. I push the accelerator. I stick my head out the window and shout as loudly as my puny voice will let me. I say, "I'm coming, Ma. I'll be right there, Ma!"

I will make the calls for her. I'll spend the night with her. I will fix her breakfast. I'll move in. I'll be good.

Heather Cox

I would be your contortionist.

If distance were to twist or separation meant to split the difference. If I could ride a telephone wire into every decibel of your voice. If your mouth were more than a dial tone. If sifting a handful of beach sand would whisper your name. If the letters you wrote to me weren't empty envelopes. If you could suture this scar, if it would silence the dissonance. If I could multiply the last minute I spent wishing, extend time for a few more regrets to fit. If to navigate distance one only need twist

Heather Cox

Letter Left on the Cusp of Our Favorite Crater

It's been weeks
of no talking, no texting, no music, no
television or Internet.

I thought we would be
the center of the universe,
the mini-moon colony on a hill.

I thought the egg crate
would have been more comfortable.

I thought the sex
would have been better.

It's been weeks
and we're still the only things
to look at.

I told you
not to forget your makeup.

We did what we could
to make this world ours,

but fingerdrawn notes in dust
are so hard to read with these
dried-out contact lenses.

This is all to say
I'm taking the [rocketship] house,

but you can have the moon.
I think we both know

who's getting the better deal here.

PS:

Whenever you decide
to fall back into our atmosphere,

I hope you land close enough
for me to collect your ashes.

Heather Cox

On the Moon,
Every Month Is December

I.

The dust begins to settle at what would be dusk,
shrinking tighter like the tucking of a blanket.
When we were younger we thought

the man in moon might
roll us in his mouth, before chewing
us like gumdrops.

Now, we fog the glass square
of window with our breath,
looking out at powdered pinnacles

and darkened craters—the pocks
like lonely scars no one ever touches
to remember. We ask ourselves

*What memories should we keep? How
should we move on?* until
the answers scramble so many times

in our mind we ignore
the questions.

II.

Beyond the absence of atmosphere
lost transmissions buzz with the worry
of travel, messages hoping to hold together,

but destined for the fate of floating fragments,
words wasted on the deaf ears
of deep space. I only wish

for the tiniest ripple of waves
from a radio, mumbles from the mouth
of a creek bed, but the wind

is bending each sound before
it slinks in my ear. I think I hear
hollow shell

or *frozen hell*, maybe *empty arms*
or *lover's swarm* or *broken charm*. I think
I feel a chill, a new depth

in the night, a snuffing out of distant light
before I'm shuttered back by
your blank breath.

Joey R. Poole

The Big, Scary Woods

Like so many other incidents in our marriage, Joanne seemed to take my inability to remove the raccoons menacing us from the fireplace as just another indication that I was not a suitable mate. If I'd been inclined to believing in signs from the Universe, as she was, I'd have taken the hint; after seven years and one day of marriage, it was clear that I was not, in fact, a suitable mate for her, nor she for me. But I was stubborn in those days, and I did not see the raccoons as a sign, and I decided to smoke them out of the chimney because as much as I wanted to leave her, I was terrified that she might up and leave me. Such is love, it seems.

A big part of the reason I didn't want to leave Joanne was that it would mean leaving Michella, Joanne's sister's kid who pretty much stayed with us because, well, her mom was a meth head. Like most three-year-olds, Michella wasn't really that sharp, but I found her company more stimulating than Joanne's. Michella was generally the happiest one in the family, and she was very excited when the raccoons came to live with us.

Michella was all jacked-up about the raccoons because her favorite book was *The Big Scary Woods*, the tale of a little raccoon named Robbie who gets lost in the big, scary woods. Every time something scares him, it turns out to be nothing at all: what he thinks is a huge monster is really just the shadow of a friendly little toad, a raging wildfire turns out to be nothing but a glowworm in the grass, and so on. In the end, Robbie reunites with his mommy and daddy and finds out he's been in his back yard the whole time, the darkness and his imagination transforming the familiar into something sinister.

The Big Scary Woods depressed me because its central theme—that there's really nothing to be afraid of in the big, scary world—was a lie bigger than the bald-faced ones we told Michella about Santa Claus and where her mommy was. But she loved the book, so I read it to her over and over, moving my finger along the words even though I had the whole thing memorized, periodically stopping to point out something about the pictures.

We were reading *The Big Scary Woods* when the real raccoons first appeared in our lives. I'd just gotten to the part where Robbie curls up to sleep thinking he's never going to see his family again when Joanne screamed so loudly I thought there must be a terrorist in the living room. She appeared suddenly in the doorway, looking down at me and Michella, talking gibberish and dancing around like she was speaking in tongues. I couldn't make out the words, but I got the gist of it: something or someone was threatening her immediate safety and the sanctity of our home, and I was either too lazy or too grossly incompetent to do anything about it.

Michella, who'd watched Joanne's outburst with the same slack-jawed wonder she displayed when she watched the show about the dancing blobs on television, suddenly began to scream. "See," Joanne yelled, "they're scaring the baby! *Do* something." The woman is unbelievable. I asked her what the matter was, closing the door behind me.

"There's ... something in the fucking chimney ...."

"We don't say those words in front of the baby," I interrupted, trying not to sound victorious even though I'd been waiting for the chance to say it for days, ever since I'd muttered *goddamnit* with Michella on my lap while I was watching a football game with my buddy Harris. Joanne had embarrassed the shit out of me with a righteous breakdown in the living room and had actually *written down a list* of things we shouldn't say in front of the kid, making sure that Harris had a copy. I hoped that Michella would chime in with a chorus of *fuck fuck fuck* like she'd done with *goddamnit*, but she just chewed on my shirt and whimpered to herself.

When I was finally able to pry Michella away and hand her to Joanne, I went into the living room and poked the fireplace screen with the blade of the ash shovel. I heard nothing, so I called for Joanne to join me.

"There's nothing in here," I said, trying to adopt a gently chiding, fatherly tone. "Must've been the wind." The chimney flue was broken, one more item on a long list of things I'd been meaning to fix since we'd bought the house, and often a strong gust would rattle it.

"I'm not stupid, Mitchell," Joanne said. "I saw them. I'm taking Michella to Grammy's. We're staying there." To make her believe me, I got down on my hands and knees and stuck my head inside the fireplace to peer up the chimney.

Before I get to what happened next, let me just say that I don't think the raccoons purposefully shat on me. I think I startled one of them who happened to have a turd standing at the ready, that I literally scared the shit out of it. Regardless of the intent, when I stuck my head in the chimney, I found myself face to face with three sets of glittering animal eyes, and a tiny ball of shit smacked me in the face and came to rest briefly in my mouth as they darted away up the chimney. I cracked my head on the fireplace in my reflex to get away, and Joanne had to drive me to the hospital, where they shaved a hole the size of a silver dollar in the crown of my head and put in four stitches. She dropped me off at the house after the hospital and took Michella to stay with her mother, Michella's Grammy, safe from the bogeymen in the chimney.

Since Joanne's mother is the one person in the world who seemed to annoy her more than I did, I figured she'd be back soon. So the next morning I called the Animal Control office, hoping to salvage a shred of my pride by having the situation taken care of before she returned. The lady who answered made it seem like I'd called her to come over and squash a spider in my bathtub. If I'd had rattlesnakes or a rabid dog on my hands, she told me, she'd send someone, but due to state budget cuts, they no longer handled raccoons. She gave me the number of a business called Critter-Gitter, but the owner's wife said he was in the middle of removing the alligators from a golf course in Myrtle Beach and wouldn't be back for a week.

I clearly wasn't up to confronting the little bastards with my head still pounding and my thoughts swimmy, so I set my e-mail for an out-of-office auto-reply, took one of Joanne's Vicodins with my coffee, and sat down in front of the TV. Sometime between *The Price Is Right* and *The Young and the Restless*, I came upon a plan that seemed downright elegant in its simplicity. I was simply going to block the fireplace. This would be a temporary solution, of course, but it would keep the little fuckers out of the house until I could figure out what to do. It would also be evidence of my proactive handling of the situation in the event of Joanne's untimely return. Maybe, if I was lucky, they'd just up and leave while I was figuring out what to do. Surely I'd given them a good scare the night before when I stuck my head up the chimney.

Just as I was finishing up with the cardboard and the duct tape, Joanne and Michella returned. Joanne surveyed my handiwork and didn't offer much in the way of comment, but Michella was enthralled. She spent the rest of the evening with her ear pressed to the cardboard covering the fireplace, tapping on it with her fingers, running away to cower behind our legs every time she heard or imagined a rustling noise. Joanne changed the bandage on my head and we laughed about me nearly cracking open my skull, which even I had to admit was pretty funny, and we all had ice cream before it was time for bed, and it was one of those rare nights when we felt like a real family, one of those times that made me understand why people crave that kind of stuff. For the bedtime story that night, Michella let me veto *The Big Scary Woods* in favor of a new selection about a farm where the pigs had a friendly rivalry with the cows and nobody ever got sent to the slaughterhouse. Halfway through the story, she fell asleep, curled on my chest, her breath warm and shallow on my collar, and I drifted off to sleep with her, warm and safe behind the cardboard barrier.

That morning I was startled awake by another of Joanne's B-movie screams and the sound of breaking glass. I jumped out of bed, dumping Michella unceremoniously onto the hardwood floor, where she, too, began to scream. When I got to the kitchen, I found that I was brandishing Michella's teddy bear like a club, and I dropped it to survey the scene. There was coffee splattered all over the far wall of the kitchen, dripping down the wallpaper, and the pot lay in shards on the floor. On the table, a loaf of bread was ripped open, the plastic bag and clumps of crusts scattered all over the table and the floor. With a growing sense of dread, I crept into the living room and saw my cardboard barricade hanging limply from the fireplace, a gaping hole chewed in one corner.

When I'd finally convinced her that the raccoons had fled back into the chimney and were sufficiently scared shitless by the shower of hot coffee they'd received not to venture back into the house, Joanne pretty much confirmed what I'd pieced together from the scene. She'd gotten up to get ready for her early shift at the hospital, and when she turned on the light, the coffeepot in hand, three raccoons had been sitting on the table, casually munching our bread. She shuddered every time she described them sitting there on their haunches, holding pieces of bread up to their faces with their little monkey hands. She swore that she'd hit one of them with the coffeepot, but she was a magnificent liar, and based on the splatter pattern, it seemed clear that the coffeepot had impacted the wall a good three feet above the top of the table.

I was sitting on the hearth, staring at the hole in the cardboard and stroking the stitches in my head when Joanne came back into the living room in her scrubs with Michella on her hip. "Cardboard? Seriously?" she asked. "They're rodents. Did you not think they were going to chew through it?"

I explained to her that raccoons were not, in fact, rodents, but she didn't find the information pertinent, and it touched off an argument that had been coming to a head for the entire length of our marriage. We trotted out pretty much every grievance we ever had against the other. She reminded me that we could have bought a better house than this fixer-upper with a broken chimney flue if I hadn't voluntarily taken a demotion and a pay cut to work from home just because I'd had one little panic attack. I reminded her that I'd supported her through nursing school and that I was free day care for her sister's kid.

One thing led to another and the slings and arrows got more vicious and personal with each round. We'd dated briefly in high school before going our separate ways and meeting up again in our twenties, and she brought up this clarinet player girl who'd given me a hand job on the back of the band bus way back then. I countered with her fake pregnancy, a melodramatic attempt to trick me into marrying her right after graduation so I couldn't go away to college, and how her own mother had sniffed it out and told me it was a hoax. Finally she brought the argument back to the issue at hand. "Cardboard!" she said, with a long-suffering sigh. "I should have known it was going to be like this. I mean, look at your daddy driving that old car around town with duct tape—duct tape!—holding the bumper on."

"You fucked your cousin," I said, ending once and for all the only argument with her in which I'd ever gotten the last word, "so don't talk to me like *I'm* trash." It was true. It had happened when they were both fourteen and drunk. He'd died a year later in a four-wheeler accident. We'd never really discussed it, but everyone in town knew it.

Though I was instantly sorry that I'd said it, a part of me marveled at the fact that for once I'd rendered her speechless. She stood there stunned for a moment and then told me she was dropping Michella off at Grammy's on her way to work, that if they came back at all, it wouldn't be until after I'd gotten rid of the raccoons. Threats to move to Grammy's were a more or less weekly component of our marriage, but they were generally theatrical and histrionic. This one she delivered so calmly that I nearly thought she might be gone for good.

"Man, there really is *nothing* to eat in here," Harris said, poking his head around in the refrigerator, which was stocked to the gills with toddler food and strange, exotic vegetables. "What is her thing now? Organic? What the fuck does that even mean? I mean, *food* is fucking organic, you know?"

"Yeah, lately it's all organic. I swear to God even the toilet paper is organic," I said. "Before that it was raw foods and before that was the macrobiotic shit." I shuddered thinking about the spaghetti sauce she used to make with beets instead of tomatoes in the midst of her macrobiotic phase.

"I liked it better way back, when she was on the low-carb thing," Harris said. "Remember that? Another steak instead of French fries? Goddamn six-egg omelets with half a pound of bacon?"

"Yep, those were the days," I admitted. "But I pretty much had the shits all the time."

Harris had gotten one of Michella's tiny applesauce jars from the fridge and was eating it with his fingers after finding out that a spoon wouldn't fit inside it. "So, uh, everything all right?" he asked, digging his finger around inside the jar. "I mean, she's not, you know, *here*."

"Seriously, I was shitting six, seven, sometimes eight times a day. Getting up in the middle of the night to shit."

"I mean, you got raccoons in the chimney. Big deal. Happens. The thing is, see," Harris said, emphatically, pausing to scoop the last of the applesauce into his mouth. "The thing, is, you know, *she's* got raccoons in *her* chimney," he said, pointing to his temple to indicate his was talking in metaphor, just in case I was stupid and couldn't pick up on it. "In fact, her whole *family's* got raccoons in the chimney, you know what I'm saying?"

Harris always seemed to perk up when Joanne and I were having problems. He happily offered marital advice gleaned from his own marriage, which had lasted only nine months but was sufficiently dramatic to teach him everything there was to know about being married. Whenever I called to ask if I could sleep on his couch, he always had steaks on the grill or oysters roasting by the time I got there. I suppose my struggles made the single life, which for Harris was a pretty lonely one of late, seem all the more appealing in contrast. If he wanted to make me jealous, it was unnecessary. Though I didn't want Joanne to leave, I was secretly very envious of both his solitude and his occasional flings that always flamed out within a month or two.

"Maybe I should just let them stay in the fireplace, live here in the house with me," I said. "They're better company anyway."

"What kind of fucking attitude is that?" Harris asked. He slipped into his parody of our high school baseball coach, whose motivational pep talks would have been more inspirational if he hadn't had a perm: "These things have come into your house, scared off your woman and your child, and *shit* in your *mouth*. And, boy, let me tell you now, there's gone come a time when you have to be a man. A *man*. And a man doesn't surrender his house to nobody. Especially not no beady-eyed, turd-slinging, glorified *rats*."

It was a rousing speech, and together we sat down to have another beer and draw up a plan. Harris's first idea was simple: we'd make sure the racoons were in the fireplace, climb onto the roof, and unload shotgun blast after shotgun blast down the chimney. This plan was sure to work but had its drawbacks in that it would be very messy, not to mention rather hard on the fireplace, which I still hoped to get operational by winter. He vetoed my idea to poison them, noting that it was not very cathartic and offered no real closure, not to mention the stench if they crawled up under the insulation in the attic to die.

What we needed was a way to flush them out and make it so they never returned, preferably by ensuring them a violent death. After some deliberation and about half a case of beer, the plan came together: I was going to light a fire in the fireplace, and Harris would stand outside with his rifle and shoot the raccoons as they fled the chimney. It seemed simple enough, and we reasoned that even if he didn't kill every single one of them, they weren't likely to take up residence again in a place where they'd been both smoked out and shot at. I planned a different story for Michella, one that involved luring them into a box and setting them free in the big, scary woods, though I debated just telling her the truth, partly because I thought she deserved it and partly because I am a terrible liar. We decided it best to wait until just before dusk, when the little nocturnal bastards first started stirring awake for the night, and in the meantime, we had a few more beers.

When it was time to roll, Harris took up his station in the back yard while I stuffed the fireplace full of newspaper doused with lighter fluid and lit it, ready with a month's worth of papers and a bunch of cardboard boxes to keep the blaze going. At first it seemed that nothing was happening, and I began to wonder if the raccoons had even been home. But as I stoked the fire a third time, I heard a shot from the back yard, followed closely by a second. At that exact same moment, Joanne came in the front door with Michella in tow. I hadn't heard her drive up. She was not happy.

"This is a *subdivision*!" she screeched. "You don't stand around in the yard and *shoot* at the house. And if somebody calls the cops, don't think we're bailing his retarded ass out of jail, either, because he still owes you money from the thing with that girl in Virginia." She was about to go on, but Harris came in the back door, the rifle slung casually in the crook of his arm.

"You said there was three of them, right?" he asked. I nodded yes. "I only saw two. Killed the first one. *Bam!* Dead before it hit the ground. Second one got away, though." Michella must have had an epiphany and pieced together for herself what was going on, because she suddenly broke out into bitter, screaming sobs for the poor raccoons.

"It's OK, sugar," Harris said, kneeling to comfort Michella, and utterly misinterpreting her cries, which began grow in intensity, "they ain't coming back. I promise you that."

Suddenly there was a commotion in the fireplace. A shower of sparks sprayed onto the hearth and out shot a tiny raccoon no bigger than a large squirrel, surely a baby, with fear in the one good eye that wasn't blackened by the ashes. It was frantic and very much on fire. We all watched in stunned silence as it scurried across the living room and tried to climb the drapes, getting about halfway up before it fell to the floor, yelping and writhing until Harris leapt into action and stomped it dead.

"Tell you what," Harris announced, "that's just not something you see every fuckin day, is it?"

"We don't say those words in front of the baby," I said, just as I saw the flames begin to lick up the curtains toward the ceiling behind him. I stood watching the fire as Harris doused it with his beer and ran to the kitchen, shouting something about water. Part of the flaming drapes drifted to the floor, catching the carpet afire. I imagined the floor burning out from under me as I stood like a tree planted in the middle of the big, scary living room, and I could hear Michella screaming from the front yard even after Joanne slammed the door for the very last time.

Travis Mossotti

Coming of Age With Aeschylus

Our playground went ahead and turned
to weed, pigeon-shit, antistrophe,
and we filled our kitchen table with
a congress of revolutionaries. One
night my brother even painted blood
on linoleum from a flap of broken knuckle
skin and smeared someone else's
to the wall using nothing but whiskey
and fruit bowl vomit—something good
was beaten to death inside that Missouri.
My enemies can laugh at what I suffered.

Travis Mossotti

Totem

—for my daughter

One day you will grow old enough to set out and climb
these Missouri hills stippled with musclewood,
blackberry, and fescue.

Climb them because they're in your blood.
Because they've been expecting you.
Because they roll like waves without breaking.

Climb to the top and watch the old red wolf
singe the air with his fogged breath. He is the fool
that unwittingly cries his kind back

into existence, into these hills which inherit us all,
paying tribute to the dead
in the currency of grass and detritus.

And even though you won't remember this,
know that your mother, pregnant with you,
carried you to work at the wolf sanctuary,

to those enclosures packed with wolves
grown weary as convicts awaiting parole,
and when they called to each other

across the winter valley
they also called to you, yet unborn,
named you first with that ancient lyric.

Francine Witte

Probably

That summer was knobby
and loose-skinned like the knuckles
of a tired old man. My father
had up and left us. Walked out
after dinner and became part
of the dark. My mother bent
into herself, babylike, never
quite straightening up. The sky
unloaded the same rain each day
at 3 o'clock. Up went the silly
umbrellas that didn't keep anything
dry. The lines on my mother's face
grew deeper and pain glowed through
her like radium.

                And probably,
my father was holed up in a cheap motel,
flickering vacancy sign. He might have been
reading the newspaper, circling the want
ads or ads for a whole new family.
Later he might have looked out
the window, bloodshot sunset
across the motel court, and later
still, most likely, sitting alone, he was
probably drinking a toast to himself.

Chris L. Terry

The Gleam

Since white is more prosperous than black, people assume that my mom came from more money than my dad. They're wrong. Dad, Henry, is the son of two schoolteachers. He grew up in Richmond, Virginia, in a black middle class neighborhood that bordered the ghetto, and repressed every base urge in a desperate attempt to distance itself from the "riffraff" mere blocks away. By the end of middle school, the conservative atmosphere had Dad harboring wild rhythm-and-blues fantasies of pulling up to his house in a Cadillac convertible, top down, saxophone music blaring, sun glinting off his processed pompadour. Anything to escape. Salvation came in 1965 when Dad, the class valedictorian, got into Harvard. He broke north.

Mom, Mary McDonnell, grew up north of Boston in Arlington, Massachusetts. When Mom and her siblings asked where they should sit for dinner, their Irish grandmother would say, "On the arse God gave ye." My memories of visiting Arlington include Catholic churches, not playing with the Carlucci girl across the street because she'd bit cousin Jo, and great-aunts with two-packs-a-day voices saying, "Christophah, I just love ya cuhly haih."

But it wasn't always that idyllic. Though Massachusetts legalized interracial marriage in the 1800s, my grandfather kicked Mom out of the family for "marrying a nigger" in 1971. None of the McDonnells spoke to Mom for a decade. I don't think Mom's family was out of step with the times, and some of Dad's relatives never forgave him for marrying a white girl, either.

In 1970, the U.S. recorded 310,000 interracial marriages where one spouse was either black or white. That seems like a lot, especially in a country where the races were so divided. But, by 2008, that number had multiplied nearly eightfold, to 2,340,000. So, you have to wonder, how did these couples, who had gone to segregated high schools, meet back then?

My friend Pat and I were in my room and Mom was down the hall, organizing her closet. The year before, the anti-drug D.A.R.E. program at school had convinced me that any illegal drugs would lead straight to jail and death, but I was beginning to question the evils of soft drugs as I heard about people that I knew using them. Pat and his older brother Kevin were two of those users. Kevin was a fifteen-year-old, long-haired metal head that Pat said would kick my ass if I didn't contain my admiration and "act cool" at their apartment. I looked up to badass Pat, too, the new kid at school with a ratty black mullet and his brother's hand-me-down rock T-shirts. Like me, Pat was in sixth grade, but he was wiser. His afternoons had a latchkey kid intrigue that I could only dream of while farting my way through trombone lessons.

I was on my bottom bunk. Pat was sprawling across the green acrylic rug, speaking in a pubescent Boston accent about a girl that had come over and blown all of his brother's friends.

"She made Sean close his eyes, but he just sat in the corner squinting, totally whacking off."

"Chris? Pat?"

It was Mom, through a wall thin enough for me to judge the tone of her and my father's nighttime mutters.

"Yeah?"

"C'mere a sec. I wanna show you guys something."

I shrugged and stood. Pat followed. Mom was at the far end of her bedroom, by Dad's stern dresser, where the Red Sox pregame show mumbled from the clock radio. Her closet door stood open and the clean room smelled musty. Glaring afternoon sun exposed dust on the high heels and peacock-patterned dresses barfing forth across the wood floor. A small trunk dented the middle of the bed. This mess rewound my mother's life to before my birth.

My parents were very private about their bedroom, an austere, beige place that made Pat's black hair, black T-shirt, and black jeans stand out like charcoal in the sand. I caught myself stepping between Pat and Mom, to block him from messing anything up. Mom pulled a slip of paper from inside the trunk's cover.

"This is my ticket to Woodstock," she said.

We stared at the blurry type and Pat flicked his bangs back, "Dude, it only cost eight bucks to get in?"

At the time, an album on cassette cost eight dollars. Twenty-five years earlier, you could dance in a field for an entire day, watching bands for eight dollars.

"Yeah," Mom said, and placed the ticket on her pillow. She kept digging through the trunk.

"Here're some pictures."

Whenever my parents were together, I was there. So, seeing photos of them in their sleek-clothed twenties, with Mom's hair ironed and Dad's 'fro bigger, yielded the same illicit excitement as the alcohol and laughter swirling in the air for the split second before they noticed me trespassing on one of their rare dinner parties.

This picture was a deeper kind of spying, to a time before Mom even knew Dad. "My roommates and I went to Amsterdam one summer," Mom said. Pat perked up at the possible drug reference.

The Polaroid showed some college-aged hippies in a dim hotel room. One woman was chunky, with giant square glasses and thick black hair that hung sideways as she lay on a bed, gazing at the floor where a pale woman in a turquoise headband sat Indian style, clamping her lips over a pencil-length joint. Some guy with a toothy grin and spray-painted-on bell-bottoms leaned in with a match. His palm cupped the flame and it looked like he was side-arming a fireball at the camera. In the background, a silver lake of mirror, a square-knobbed dresser, a distended bell-bottom leg nudging into the frame's right side.

Mom pointed to the woman with the glasses.

"That's Lila, who taught me how to say 'shit' in Arabic. *Hudda.*"

I'd heard of Lila and I'd heard *hudda* before. Pat nodded at the swear word.

Then she pointed at the woman with the joint, "That's me."

I'd never heard that before. My eyes bugged and I was drawn in to look, bumping heads with Pat, who had done the same. His hair had the sour stink of cigarettes in wall-to-wall carpeting.

I looked from Hippie Mom to Now Mom, a bit rounder, strawberry-blond hair wilder, in the turquoise shirt with the homemade butterfly sewn over the hole that had landed it on the irregular rack.

"Who are the guys, Mom?"

"Oh, just some guys we met while we were out."

Her tone was casual, but this was the woman who wouldn't stop at the gas station when there were men standing around by the garage. She changed the subject fast, whipping out a new photo.

"Here's Jimi Hendrix getting out of a VW bug on the autobahn in Germany."

The Polaroid had been taken from the top of a C-curve in the road. Hendrix was midstride in a green Army parka, paisley dashiki and crumbling blue jeans that held tight to his skinny thighs. His 'fro made him a flower, growing from the door of the orange car.

Pat gasped. I asked, "Wow, did you talk to him?"

The guitars from Dad's Hendrix records howled through the house most weekend afternoons.

"Of course I did."

Had Pat's mom ever met Hendrix? We looked from each other's faces back to my mother. She laughed and shook the photo, "That's your father. You don't recognize your own father?"

I knew Dad as a khakis-and-polo-shirt type of guy, whose metabolism had caught up with his Frito-Lay eating habits, resulting in a decent paunch. He looked nothing like the lithe rock 'n' roll machine stepping out of that Volkswagen.

The radio went to a wine cooler commercial. As Pat laughed at me and I laughed in embarrassment, Mom dug back into her loot and broke in with the "Oop" noise that she's always made when surprised. She emerged with a little plastic bag, calcified like old Scotch tape, with a smeary black ball in the corner.

"This is hash that I stuck in my sock and brought home."

Pat and I gaped and my stomach bottomed out. It was my first time seeing drugs and they were a vortex, sucking in the whole room. What if Bussy Adams, the cop who had taught my D.A.R.E. class, drove by and saw us? Mom pointed her elbow forward then overhanded the baggie into the basket-weave trash can under the window. Pat's hungry eyes followed its arc until it disappeared amongst the used tissues. Mom pointed out the window at the tan house next door.

"You know, Patsy and Russell used to grow grass on their porch. When I was pregnant with you, me and Dad went to a party there and they were smoking it."

"You didn't, did you?" I knew that pregnant ladies couldn't even drink beer because it would mess up their baby.

"No, of course not," said Mom. "Well, not then."

While we were talking about D.A.R.E., Mom had said, "Don't even try to do drugs. We'll know," and I'd believed her. And now I knew how she'd know. Everything I'd been raised to believe was wrong was actually normal—Hippie Mom in Amsterdam, gray-haired Russell smoking a canoe-sized pipe—but it made Pat think we were cool. He bounced on his feet, peeking out the window.

Drugs didn't always ruin your life. Sometimes they lead to families with two children and a beagle. For the last twelve years, there had been drugs feet away from where I slept, and I'd turned out fine, even if I sucked at soccer and girls didn't come over to blow me and my friends. And I was about to be in junior high, and I'd actually seen drugs, which was a bigger deal than Dad pointing out the sick-sweet smell of them during the Aerosmith concert at Boston Garden.

Mom dismissed us. I sat on my bed again. Pat was back on the rug, dandruff bright on the shoulders of his Led Zeppelin shirt. "Dude, is your mom still in there?" He grinned and his chin zits stretched red. "Let's go dig that hash outta the trash."

"Nah, dude, she'd know."

Even if I was old enough to see that drugs weren't always bad, I was young enough to still believe in the omnipotence of Mom.

During the summer of 1967, Dad listened to Simon and Garfunkel's "Parsley, Sage, Rosemary, and Thyme" every day. In eighth grade, I taped Dad's record after hearing the Lemonheads cover "Mrs. Robinson." We played it in the moving truck while driving our family's things from no-job Boston to cheap-rent Richmond. We were on the interstate in Connecticut, going just below the speed limit in the right lane, when "The 59th St. Bridge Song" came on and Dad chuckled. I looked up from my Sherlock Holmes book, wondering what had drawn laughter from this man, who had done the beginning of the drive in white-knuckled silence. He turned down the radio and spoke in the candid tone that he reserved for old stories.

"Once, I was making out with a girl to this album and that first line," Dad looked away from the road for a second before jerking his head back and cutting the wheel left, "'Slow down, you move too fast/

You got to make the moment last,' came on and we stopped kissing and started laughing."

Dad smiled at his memory, now almost thirty years old. I laughed, too, to show that I'd made out before and knew what was up, then looked out the windshield, realizing that the woman in the story wasn't Mom. Sure, Dad's old prom photos proved that he had dated before, but those Motown-looking girls were abstractions from a different black-and-white time, and I couldn't imagine them kissing my father.

Not a week later, our family drove through Dad's old neighborhood in Richmond. It was hard to believe that these failing blocks of dead grass and plywood windows had raised my father, the king of our home. He pointed to a once-grand rowhouse, now chipping paint "That's where Martha Birdsong lived. We went to junior prom together and Grandpa rode in the back seat. He said, 'I don't want to be a grandfather just yet.'"

This wasn't the first ex's house that we had passed. Mom shifted in her seat, "I think your father had a girlfriend on every block."

Later, we stopped at Dad's Aunt Edith's shotgun house. Edith was pushing ninety but still tall and imposing, with glasses and wiry white hair. My sister and I looked forward to seeing Edith because she'd give us twenty-dollar bills from the horse track, and, more importantly, she'd tease Dad, which was especially welcome after the move.

We sat on a hard couch in her bare-floored living room, smelling liniment and cigars. Edith faced us in her throne, a steel-blue armchair, sun-bleached by the nearby porch door. Mom said, "Edith, Henry made a point to drive us by all of his old girlfriends' houses."

Dad rolled his eyes and looked out at Idlewood Avenue.

"Don't you worry, Mary," Edith said in her Southern growl ("Doanchoo worreh Mayreh"). "They all fat grandmothers by now."

The four of us laughed. Dad kept looking at the summer day outside of the stuffy house. I hoped Mom felt better, but hadn't Edith just said that Mom and Dad were the same age as a bunch of fat grandmothers?

In 1969, Dad had graduated Harvard and been accepted to Yale Law, when he avoided the draft by joining the Coast Guard as a recruiter. The U.S. was integrating the armed forces and needed a black man to bring in black troops so they could die in Vietnam like everyone else.

Dad was against the war, but if he took this recruiter job, he'd be sworn in as an officer, and the farthest from home that he'd be sent would be the end of the Orange Line train. All he had to do was put on his whites and try to rustle up business for Uncle Sam. Law school could wait for a couple years.

Dad stopped off at a lot of bars while working. If someone asked about his uniform, he'd say, "I'm a recruiter."

The local hippies would always be skeptical. They'd cock an eyebrow while asking, "You want to send me off to Vietnam?"

"No, no, I don't," Dad would answer, using his middle finger to wipe a line of condensation off the side of his whiskey glass.

"Then why have you got the job, maaan?" the hippie would ask, raising his shoulders and voice.

"Because if I have this job, I don't have to go off to Vietnam … maaan."

"My man," the hippie exclaims and claps Dad on the shoulder. "Let me buy you a drink."

"No," says Dad, hand up, then pointing like in the recruiting posters, "Let Uncle Sam buy YOU a drink."

They both laugh. Later, Dad becomes one of many men to scrub puke and whiskey out of Coast Guard whites.

Since a black Coast Guard officer was a new idea in the '60s, Dad benefited from the fact that the grooming regulations were written with straight-haired men in mind. Straight hair succumbs to gravity, and Afro hairstyles were not taken into account. All of the rules were about how far *down* hair could go, but nothing about how far *up* or *out*. In compliance, Dad trimmed his 'fro up around his neck and picked it out over his ears. When his superiors tried to send him to the barber, he showed them the rule book.

The Coast Guard wanted it to look like they were working to integrate, but they didn't monitor my father's progress. That's a good thing, because, in the two years that Dad recruited, only one person joined on his account. Says Dad, "He must have really wanted to join when he ran into me, because I tried to talk him out of it."

There was a dive bar that Mom and her crew liked. While its patrons lived in progressive Cambridge, Massachusetts, the décor was from backwards times: wood-paneled walls, dead flies in the jukebox, a stained-glass beer lamp over the pool table and a couple sticky booths across the linoleum floor from the bar.

With the exception of Lila (*hudda*), Mom's crew was comprised of other white women from her Catholic college. They would stand in a corner, joking, sipping glasses of beer, and eyeing the door by the jukebox, noting who came and went. Sometimes they'd laugh extra hard then scan the room, like single people do in places like that. They were regulars. They knew most of the hippie faces: women with ironed hair and turquoise jewelry, guys with walrus mustaches and John Lennon glasses. Mom and her friends had a rule: if a new guy came in, one of them had to ask him for a dime for the jukebox.

One night, the bar door closed behind a black guy with a high-flying 'fro and white military clothes that glowed in the smoke-hazed air. One of Mom's friends snorted into her beer. Another elbowed her, "Get'm, Mary."

It was 1970. The hippies knew that racism was bad, but most of the hippies were white. This new racial equality was more of a theory than a way of life. Was Mom interested in this black guy or was she just following protocol with her friends? What would they say if she dated him? Some truly wouldn't care. She'd be able to tell that some did care by the way that, over and over, they made a point to say that they didn't. If she got together with a black guy, it would prove that she was even more progressive than the others. It would be a middle finger to the fake hippies and her father, who called her favorite folk singer Richie Havens "that toothless nigger."

Dad, still in uniform, had just gotten back from signing up for an Encounter Group. Encounter Groups were hippie group therapy where people got together to talk about their feelings. Says Dad, "It was a popular thing to do back then, and me and my roommate used to go to try and pick up chicks."

By the time Mom got to Dad, he was leaning over the bar, ordering a whiskey. She reached out and tapped his upper arm just as he was bringing his elbow back for his wallet. When he felt her finger, he jumped and drew his arm in like a T-rex, wheeling around with the wallet clenched in his fist. Then he smiled at the sight of her blue eyes. She laughed and said, "Do you have a dime for the jukebox? This is our bar, you know," she motioned back to her friends, who suddenly stopped staring at her, "and all new guys have to give us a dime for the jukebox."

Once Dad saw that "us" was a bunch of attractive women he said, "Well, I'm a new guy," and fished in his pocket for a coin. "And I'll pay the toll ... if you dance with me."

The big hits that summer were Eric Clapton singing about stealing George Harrison's wife in "Layla," the Kinks discussing a virgin's champagne-soaked rendezvous with a transvestite in "Lola," and "Sex Machine" by James Brown. I don't like to match any of those songs up with my parents' first dance, so let's say that they threw on a song by another young Bostonian, Bonnie Raitt, cut a rug, then sat down with a beer.

Days after Dad left his recruiter job, a friend in the office told him that the Coast Guard had already changed their grooming regulations to include a ruler test for everyone, especially those with kinky hair.

Rick Marlatt

The Lesson

Behind the fervent torch of his cigarette my father warned me once,
those corn rows better be truer than an eagle's sheer at sunrise
or your grandpa will climb out of his grave and teach you a lesson.

If the frosty-haired shuffler I remember clenching his walker
went to all that work—becoming undead, cursing through root and grime
squinting at the world like an earth-smattered monster—

I'd want the lesson to be pretty damn good.
I still can't water ski, bake bread, or understand war. Chopsticks are still
a mystery, as are lawn care, small talk, and good knots.

I'd drive him crazy with questions about the Dust Bowl, the Depression;
did he have one of those hats?

Things might be safer for him down in the soft cradle
where he doesn't have to reconsider or reimburse, where he doesn't have
to share the secrets to those foil dinners I ate at Scout camp when men

with colossal beards and godlike bellies wrapped ground beef with carrots
and potatoes inside their silver shells and flipped them into the embers,
faithful of the invisible heat inside,

faithful that all the questions would be answered, like what is
this tradition of man, what is this sky-locked constancy that balances us,
what story burns inside our bodies in the dark?

Rick Marlatt

An Apology for Not Waking You

It's as good a time as any to tell you
my thing was to creep into my parents' room,
to let the quiet rumble of their snores
surround me in a warm wavelength.
I'd stare into their faces until I had to blink,
until my mind hacked itself
into seeing different life forms lying there.
For good measure, it was necessary
to carefully peel back their eyelids, to watch
dreams create themselves in soft circles.
One night I was home alone,
old enough for a leaner's permit
but not enough to coordinate an attack
on whomever opened the front door.
It wasn't the easy footsteps
or the nonchalant shifting of silverware
that paralyzed me on the long mauve sofa.
It was the eternity between breaths
I could barely calculate.
My defense was to stretch my eyelids
into the depths of my forehead,
to lose myself in the darkness.
In the dark we sail numb and anonymous
on a shared vessel for the living and dying.
I know you wanted to be perched
in your reading chair at the very moment
the sour light soaked through the window,
tangled up in the frayed wedding blanket,

taking your coffee outside,
finger curled around a cigarette,
listening to the finches rifle up their chatter.
Forgive me again as I tame
the tall noises of the night.
Pardon my patrol to preserve
the perfect silence in your parted lips.
Like any cunning and beautiful bird,
you'll know precisely when it's time to rise.

Michael Levan

Self-Portrait
in a Plywood Carnival Cutout

Dogpatch Gift Shop, Lake Ozark, Missouri

I could have shed my shape easily

       like water pouring from pitcher to glass,

glass to beads slipping down chin

       then summer-tanned throat, water which never

settles on one identity when there are

       so many ways to be itself. Isn't that a promise

I could have made to myself? To peek my head

       again and again through wooden ovals,

pushing from darkness to sun so suddenly

       there'd be no way to know whether light

or each chance at being new had me

       crumple to my knees, clutch my eyes tight,

blink them open as whoever I could be?

Maybe a black-and-white clad prisoner,

ankle-chained to the next man, leaning

shovel into dirt heap as shotgunned guard, bloodhound,

and my every mistake stood there at the roadside.

Or a no-shoed, knee-patched yokel,

corncob pipe in my threadbare vest's pocket

and triple-X'ed jug at my hip, sitting atop an ass.

I was *heading fer home* as the stocky letters

drawn in mountain-stretching clouds

declared. Or even a golden-skinned skier with two choices:

grip towline hard back to shore

as sharkfin tailed close in the boat's wake

or let go and fall back into the dark

because there's always time for a man to ask forgiveness,

to be cleansed, to find how he fits this life once more.

Dacora Digna c. 1954

Becky Hagenston

Puppet Town

Once there was a town where everyone wore a puppet on their right hand, as decreed by law, moral code, and common sense. Many years earlier (before anyone could remember), a man came through town wearing a burlap sack on his right hand, with two buttons sewn on for eyes. There were paintings in the town's historical society depicting the man thrusting out his sacked hand as if to hold back the wind, the townspeople on their knees before it.

A local woman recorded the events in her diary, also on display in the historical society. "I am pure," shouted the puppet, in a high and reedy voice, "and because I am pure, so is he." He gestured at the man. "We live honestly and humbly." Then the puppet dipped into a giant wooden box and reappeared with tiny burlap sacks clutched in his burlap mouth. He tossed them into the crowd, and the townspeople cheered.

Before the puppet-prophet came to town, there had been much sin and licentiousness, gambling and fornicating. But with the coming of the puppets, everything changed. At the craps tables, the puppets refused to play, spitting the dice across the room. Even the left-handed gamblers quailed before the watchful button-eyes, eventually putting on their hats and going home. The saloon closed down within three months and reopened as a burlap and button store. The prostitutes grew sore from the rough burlap spankings; their customers grew tired of the puppets' high chattering voices preaching against sin. When the puppets went on this way, it was impossible to interrupt them.

Wives were pleased to learn that the puppets were excellent cooks and helpmeets. A wife's puppet was always ready to assist her with a hot pan, offer recipe advice, or push the mop. Sometimes a husband would come home from work and find his wife sitting at the kitchen table, laughing at something her puppet was saying. When a man and his wife were alone in the bedroom, their puppets would ask politely to be placed in a bureau drawer.

Years passed, and the town became more isolated as fewer and fewer of its citizens ventured beyond it. The puppets encouraged this, cautioning the humans about the dangers of a world where both hands were naked to perform unmentionable acts of depravity. (The puppets would refuse to mention these acts, shaking their heads and rattling their eyes.) The puppets were made of blue felt now, rather than burlap, and their eyes resembled human eyes, and their mouths were wide and red. Some of them had teeth.

More and more, husbands and wives would retreat to their bedrooms and find that their puppets wanted to talk about politics and puppet rights, rather than go silently into the bureau. When the birthrate began to drop, the puppets ordered the husbands and wives to sleep together, even though the puppets hovered above and around them, and sometimes (it was whispered) asked to take part.

Every once in a while, a young man and a young woman would sneak off to the forest outside of town and remove their puppets and stare into each others' eyes, four naked hands fumbling, and speak to each other in their real voices. Many of them had forgotten what their real voices sounded like. Sometimes they fell in love, but usually they left the forest feeling annoyed and ashamed, their puppets tsk-tsking at them as they drove home.

And sometimes a teenager would rip the puppet off and throw it on the ground, vowing never to listen to it again, only to realize hours or minutes later that they had no idea how to live without that small, high voice, those stern plastic eyes. "I'm sorry," they would murmur, stroking the blue felt. "Please forgive me."

The puppets usually did, but not always.

And so, as time went on, a kind truck driver on the El Paso-to-San Francisco route knew to expect hitchhikers on the highway outside of Puppet Town: all teenagers—boys and girls—all with the same look of terror on their faces, their right hands shoved into jacket pockets. Sometimes they wept softly, and the truck driver offered them Kleenex but didn't pry. They spoke in whispers. When they thought he wasn't looking, he would catch them staring at their pale right hands, their mouths slack with fear or wonder, moving their fingers as if pushing invisible buttons.

Sometimes they left him at the first pit stop, and sometimes they made it all the way to his destination. It was always a relief to leave them, to honk his horn and wish them well. The only time they seemed perfectly normal—like himself at sixteen, far from home and ready for adventure—was when they were in his rear-view mirror, waving good-bye.

Ryan Gannon

Five Unconventional Uses for Marshmallows

1.

Make a bouquet on the tips of skewers. Invite everyone at the singles'
mixer to take a whiff. The "fun" woman who's wearing a thrift-store
pleated skirt and cowboy boots will bite down on one, not realizing
the skewers have pointed tips. The roof of her mouth will heal, but
not until after a burning infection, one doctor's visit, and two weeks
of antibiotics. Offer to take her out for drinks, but she can't—alcohol
could either "A: cause the infection to flare up" or "B: screw up her
meds." Don't return her phone calls when she decides she feels better;
too much time has passed, and you've lost your motivation.

2.

Bait the raccoon that's been living in your attic by leaving a trail of
those stale Swiss Miss cocoa-floaters from the ladder with the pull-
string door, straight down the stairs and into your bathtub. Drop a
stereo playing Queen into the water while it's still plugged in. Pay for
the electrician to run a new grounded line from the breaker box to the
bathroom. Just lie when he asks you what smells so bad in there—like
wet hair on fire. Don't tell him how that doesn't make any sense. Keep
humming the melody to "Don't Stop Me Now" as you scrawl your
signature across the check. This will keep him from asking again.

3.

Make your mother a necklace of those multicolored miniatures you
see in holiday desserts, specifically the chocolate church windows she
used to make when you were a kid. The string should be edible, too—a
thin piece of licorice will do. She'll wear it while you have coffee at

her kitchen table, nibbling at the puffy fruit-flavored squares until the sugar sticks to her neck. Don't worry, she won't ask why, won't bring up your losing custody battle for the kids. She won't even be upset that it's her birthday. She'll place her hand over yours, and her skin will feel thin, like linen, and you'll tell her the job search is going well. She'll nod, work up a slanted smile, and grip your fingers. She may ask you to get a haircut.

4.

Microwave a bowl of mallows and allow yourself a brief grin as they bubble up and pop while oscillating on the glass tray. Apply the molten mess to your bare chest immediately. Even though nobody's watching, you'll feel like someone is, so don't wince at the heat. Go outside and lie in the grass in your back yard. It's late spring—the sun is hot in the afternoon, despite the breeze. The mallows resolidify. If you lie still enough, you'll hear the ants before you see them as they make their way from sandy hill to bent and bowed blades of neglected grass. Don't wriggle when they start biting, crawling over the gooey surface in neat, circulating single-file, their little pincers clack-clacking as they pick you apart and take the pieces home. When you've had enough, go inside, shower off, and try not to look in the mirror. You won't like what you see.

5.

Wake up with a sore throat because as it turns out, ants carry disease, too. Eat several mallows, whatever you have left in the cupboard; a news website says the gelatin soothes inflammation. Find out that this is only temporary, like sucking on a lozenge. Fight the cold for a week and go back to work the following Monday, and skip looking for a new job. When people ask what's wrong with you, arch your brow in confusion. Pretend nothing's happened, but then buy a fresh bag of Jet-Puffed from the dollar store on your way home, just in case. Repeat this process as needed, but keep it to yourself because you've never been good at explaining this sort of thing, anyway.

W. Todd Kaneko

Junkyard Dog Says Everything's Gonna Be All Right

*Don't worry about a thing. Tonight, tonight, everything's gonna be all right
…. You have to pay the cost to be the boss. Don't try to do nothing wrong.
Everything's gonna be all right on a Saturday night.*
—*Junkyard Dog, professional wrestler*

It's *Saturday Night's Main Event,*
where everyone knows the Junkyard Dog
has a headbutt that makes his mother
so proud that she dances to "Another One
Bites the Dust." I am fifteen in 1985,
too uneasy to sit near that girl
who draws horses in art class.
Junkyard Dog has vanquished so many
titans with that unbreakable headbutt—
Big John Studd, King Kong Bundy,
Kamala the Ugandan Giant—so tonight,
that soft-bellied sucker doesn't stand
a chance against JYD. I am home
on Saturday night, watching television
instead of stealing beer with my friends,
instead of sneaking an arm around a girl
who might sit behind me in biology.
Junkyard Dog lets that dude punch him
in the face, then blows him out of the ring
with a headbutt. My father tells me
a man never throws a first punch, so I think
about knocking a man out with my skull,

then making out with that shy girl
from my typing class. Junkyard Dog gets down
on all fours and shows his teeth—chomps
at the dusky stadium air and his mother
shakes her fists. Somewhere that night,
there must have been a girl stuck
at home, maybe watching people dance
on television, maybe wondering about
the precision of her feet, about a boy
who holds one hand to his forehead
when the algebra teacher opens his mouth.

W. Todd Kaneko

Ain't No Cage Can Hold Mad Dog Sawyer

My father had no bedtime stories,
so he told me about that fabled brawl
down South where Mad Dog Sawyer
prowled the backwoods with his mouth
full of rabies, where pain calls the animal
out from beneath a man's breastbone.
Tommy "Wildfire" Rich, decked out
in ivory and gold, that flaxen boy
who filled every stadium with his name,
thrown into that cage with the Mad Dog
to duke it out one last time. They called it

"The Last Battle of Atlanta"—Buzz Sawyer
furious behind chain-link, Wildfire throwing
elbows and dropkicks, body bejeweled
by blood and rust for the Mad Dog.
That cage was slick with juice,
sick with teeth and hammerfists,
the Mad Dog cackling like fire
for a man's carcass. I used to dream
about the Mad Dog's yard, a ring of steel
and razor wire where a man can show off
his scars and howl for someone to beat on.
I still see things at night—my father
shirtless in the parking lot, a beer pressed
to his chest, my mother's shadow
astride a motorcycle, rabbits tumbling
headless through the yard.

☾

Pain is a chain of syllables that rises
from the gut and spills from the tongue.
There is no prison like a man's skeleton,
no collar like the bones surrounding
a man's heart as he pushes his belly out
at the darkness, as he batters himself
against the cage, as he wishes
he had different stories to tell.

Erin Elizabeth Smith

Alice in Knoxville

Sometimes the other side
of the glass is nothing

but Tennessee, the redbuds
opening like viscera

against its interstates.
I watch the hostas

shoot their egret heads
from the green and puzzle

through the drunks
who sing a fiddled ballad

as if Dionysus himself
first strummed them

to their stupor. It's April,
that witty month that breathes

like a woman grasping
her knees after the long chase.

Each lawn comes up like a chessboard,
and I maneuver my way through,

thinking some places are never
the Oxford homes we grew tall in

but from the hills of the fort
those river boats could be Charlie's

and it could be my name
the gray birds call out.

Court Walsh

Natasha on the Neva

Why did Natasha cry "Pomortne!?" Because she was falling.

Why did she say "Pomortne" instead of "Help me"? Because she was Russian. She had been leaning over the edge of a stone bridge in Moscow on a December evening in 1904.

What finally arrested her fall? Ice.

Ice? The Neva River had frozen over.

What was the Neva doing in Moscow? It had done a river swap with the Volga.

How cold was it on this night? Very cold.

Did Natasha become deceased from the sudden stop? Of course not.

What did she say then when she struck the ice? *Govno*, which is Russian for "shit."

What were additional reasons for her distress at the moment? She had landed on a larder of beluga caviar she had been told to deliver to Count Rozaharpski. The black gooey eggs were smeared all over the ice. Also, her employer, Dmitri Dezhnikov, who ran one of the city's most exclusive restaurants, would not be pleased.

What did Natasha see upon gaining her footing? Stars.

When, upon further scrutiny, she correctly identified the Milky Way, to what did she compare it? A dairy churn whirling around the night sky.

What prevented her from further use of her poetic license? A figure had appeared on the bridge, a man.

Did the man ask her in Russian if she was all right down there? Yes.

Why did she swoon when he ran down and took her in his arms? Because he was preposterously handsome. The tips of his mustache tickled her cheek.

When she asked the man if he liked caviar, what conversation then ensued?
Doesn't everyone? the man said.
You might as well take some. There will be a shortage during the revolution.
Revolution?
It's coming. You needn't ask why. I know these things.

What other things suddenly came to her mind? Ripe-smelling, hamster-eating Mongol hordes murdering their way across the country a long time ago. In the not-to-distant future, gold domes of Orthodox churches all sooty from the exhaust of black Volvos.

To what could Natasha attribute her newfound certainty and prescience? She didn't know, though she thought it might have had something to do with falling.

When the man placed his hand on Natasha's babushka, what did he feel? Blood.

How did the man reply when Natasha told him "Hands off buster, I've heard that one before"? That he was a doctor. That he wouldn't dream of molesting her. That, furthermore, he was affianced.

When Natasha allowed the man to continue his examination, what did he utter under his breath? That her lump was bigger than a gooseberry. That she might have suffered a severe concussion.

Did she think this was all horseshit? The possibility occurred to her, though not exactly in that form because Russian has no equivalent for that idiom in English.

What kind of doctor are you? Natasha asked.
I'm Doctor Zhivago.
Not Yuri Zhivago?
How did you know my name?
As I said before: I just know these things.

What else did she see that caused her to swoon a second time? The Siberian permafrost, in a century or so, turning into a gigantic swamp by the extraction of fossil fuels, and the release of millions of tons of methane into the atmosphere so that people might never see the stars again.

What was transpiring in the heavens at this moment? The Milky Way continued to be dazzling, and dazzling too was its congenital twin, a galaxy made entirely of antimatter in an alternate universe.

Did these cosmic events affect what next transpired? Not a whit.

Kelly Goss

In Terms of a Whale

You have a big overgrown garden in the summertime. You walk between the rows barefoot, stepping over vines and getting in deep to reach the zucchini, the yellow squash.

When you come back to me you smell like green beans and your fingers are prickly with the tiny hairs of vegetables.

Sometimes I end up behind you on the highway, your green truck, and I look through the rain-spattered windshield to see if you're on the phone, if you're singing. When you exit into the city I wave and keep going, though you don't see.

We go to dinner at my parents' place, and when they kiss in front of us, you turn to me and whisper, "I want to end up like that."

I would take a trip with you to Yellowstone if you asked.

I keep speaking in terms of you, *you*, as if doing otherwise would set me adrift, cast me to sea like a lonely whale. I watch the shimmery haze above a parking lot full of cars and get dizzy.

Whales breathe through a blowhole on the top of the head, which allows them to become almost completely submerged in water. Blowhole shapes differ among species and may help with identification.

On our last trip we went on a whale-watching boat. Instead of scanning the waters you grasped the rails and told me you were in trouble, that you'd thought about having an affair with Jolene from work.

I tasted silver in my mouth.

I often come to your house after work to find you in the shower, whistling. I peek at you through the glass door, watch you try to pick stray hairs off your chest.

Whales, unlike most animals, are conscious breathers. If they were to fall into what we call a "deep sleep," they would drown.

The other night I had a dream that my belly was huge, covered in stretch marks, that I felt a kick.

When your seventeen-year-old cat Iggy died we found her fur all over the place, like a little trail, and you cried for the first time in front of me.

Sometimes the ordinary of a relationship gets mistaken for boredom. Sometimes you just can't help it.

We were kissing when we heard the blowhole of a whale, that splattering breath, but we didn't stop. There was no need to identify it.

I admit that I was once attracted to a homeless man. He had clear skin and dark eyes, hair that tucked behind his ears. He sat with his dog and when he smiled at me it sent a shock right down to my stomach. Instead of risking it I gave him my ChapStick, his lips where mine had been.

When we're in bed with the window open I suck on your fingers, taste ripe cherry tomatoes.

Whales are descendants of land-living mammals of the Artiodactyla order. They took to the sea fifty million years ago. They have four-chambered hearts. They hear through their throats.

I don't know if there's ever a time you know something for certain. You have to ask questions to figure it out.

When we lose power at night there's a beeping sound, a surge protector that wakes us up. It always gets me first and I look to see how long it takes you to stir. After it finally turns off I stay awake, restless.

I think about leaving land behind, too.

Gary Leising

Squids Will Be Squids

is all I can think to say to you now,
having watched your marriage fall apart,
having offered sympathy throughout,
having tried to advise both you and him
on how to approach therapy,
each other, the tarnished silver cup
of love from which you drink no more.
Months into this, you will ask, "Why me?"
and I will not offer my shoulder or
some fake psychology, but I'll just say,
"Squids will be squids,"
because, of course, he is a squid,
cephalopod of the order *Teuthida*
with a distinct head, bilateral symmetry,
a mantle, and arms, eight arms
arranged in pairs and two,
usually larger, tentacles. This taxonomy
does not explain why he spent
two years pretending to love you,
nor does the squid's presence in cuisines
from Portugal to the Philippines offer a justification
for the now omnipresence in his life
of this "Nancy" person. The only
inedible parts of a squid are
the beak and gladius, and I do not know
what the gladius is.
The beak, however, is hard and pointed,
and ranges in size from miniscule, barely visible,

to almost 2.5 inches long. Sounds small,
but when its point digs into your skin,
hooks on a finger, hangs in your lung
or heart or spleen, or rips circles around
the lining of your stomach every day,
the pain is unbearable. Even
to the smallest one you say,
"Stop being a squid, squid.
Once you had the soft lips of a human."

Gary Leising

A Sparrow in His Shopping Cart, Its

beak crushed, neck broken when it slammed
into the old man's picture window, landed
in the manicured garden he worked in each morning,
the old man tucked it in his jacket pocket,
too hard on his knees to stand, walk it to the trash,
come back to kneel at the two miniature rosebushes
and get back to trimming. No bugs on the bird yet,
so it must have crashed right before he came out,
how could he know, his hearing so gone
he's given up on knowing much of the world,
his trust in what he touches or sees.
The sparrow's body feels too light for its size,
its feathers too rigid for something that could fly.
He trims the bushes and smoothes the dirt and mulch
around each plant. His day goes on. Later,
he searches his jacket for the shopping list, afraid
his slippery memory has let some staple disappear.
But the list, he's forgotten it, finds the also-forgotten
bird instead. Nothing to do with it but toss it
in the basket, shop for what he thinks he needs:
cheap coffee, bread, and thin-sliced deli meat.
He tells the cashier he'll be back. She doesn't care.
Like everyone else she eyes the bird
but won't make eye contact with him. The bird
in his basket. He'll push the cart all the way home
though what he bought is light enough to carry.
And the bird, he carried that all morning,
could carry it with him all day if only he knew
what he'd do with it at noon, at dinner,
or, after sunset, in those hard, unyielding hours.

Mark Wisniewski

Intentions

Check out the size of these cabins, Bill said, but there was no one in his F-150 to listen. There rarely was. There'd been his father, but his father had long since passed. It was just him, Bill.

Bill with no luck, he muttered, and then there it was, the professor-lady's driveway. He hung the right, cut the engine, engaged the brake, sipped the last of his joe, and flung the cup at the passenger side while shouldering open his door. Quilts, she'd said. How could there be two hundred?

He walked past her Prius, stood on her concrete porch. She didn't have cheap siding—those were actual logs. He knocked and her door rattled and opened. She was older than she'd sounded, but she had a good face.

You made it, she said.

Was there some question, he said.

There's been a red flag warning, she said. Plus a neighbor who called mentioned a fire not far from here—I was sure they wouldn't let you through.

Oh, I got through, Bill said. A fire? he thought. How could he not have known?

Good then, she said, and she shut the door behind him, and then he couldn't remember having stepped inside, as if, for a moment there, he'd blacked out. She wore a lavender robe, corduroy with very wide spaces between the ridges and, he guessed, fairly small panties.

So I have these quilts, she said.

And you say you can't get rid of 'em? he asked, to be nice.

I set out a dozen or so for the recyclers, but they didn't take them.

You actually have recycling up here?

Unofficially, she said. People on this road and I pay a concern in Sacramento to send up a truck every month.

I see, Bill said. He could almost taste restaurant-quality food. He would probably go with ribs and steak fries. But what I don't understand, he said, is why everyday people—I mean people not in the recycling business—would turn down a good quilt. Of course I figure these are clean? And, you know, thick?

Most of them never used at all, she said. And most stuffed with goose down! It's a mystery to me, too, why no one wants them, but I'm to the point that I can no longer tolerate thinking about them.

He nodded—the response he believed a male professor might give—and in this silence, with nothing more to say about quilts in general, he felt stupid.

I suppose you want to see them, she said.

Ma'am?

Before you commit to taking them? I suppose you want to see them?

Sure, he said, but then he thought: Isn't a quilt a quilt?

Come, she said, and she led him through her living room, which had no TV, past a bedroom with a king-sized bed, unmade but firm-looking, the kind you could really screw on, then through a kitchen stocked with wicker baskets of oranges and garlic cloves and one impossibly large grapefruit. She let one hand float toward him and said, You probably noticed I don't sleep with any.

Men? he wanted to say, but again he nodded, again, he hoped, like a professor might.

Then she had him outside, slamming her back door so hard it wound up ajar—a problem he could fix lickety-split. She kind of glided, on Chinese slippers, he noticed only now, to an aluminum shed where her yard gave way to woods that thickened and widened and joined the national park. He smelled no smoke. Had she bullshitted about the fire? Her shed's corners were rusty thanks to a bad roof job, and it was unlocked, and he slid its door open.

Criminy, he said.

Right? she said. It's possible that no one in the world except you and me knows what two hundred quilts in one shed look like.

It's mind-boggling, he said, his best crack at an assessment she'd admire.

But by the look on her face now, he'd just messed with her mind. Or maybe the sight of the quilts had? Her fingernails, painted gold, raked at the scalp beneath the bed-head section of her frosted hair, and her face looked even better than it had at first glance, age spots and wrinkles and all.

You mind my asking? he said.

Pardon?

How you come up with two hundred quilts?

Her eyes screwed up like she'd just shot tequila. People? she said. *Give* them to me.

He nodded.

For any particular reason? he asked.

Her lips parted, and she pursed them. He was sure she'd prefer if he didn't ask questions.

Finally she answered: I'm a poet.

Huh, he said. I thought you was a professor.

Well, that, too. But they made me a professor because I wrote poems. Because I *published* poems, I should probably say. And part of my job as a professor was to read my poems at ... readings—you know, in front of other people—and for the past thirty—actually, it's now thirty-two years—pretty much every time I've read my work publicly, someone's come up from the audience and given me a quilt.

I understand, Bill said, even as he thought: Weird stuff.

Then she and he stood still.

To keep you warm? he asked.

Beg pardon?

They'd give you a quilt to keep you warm?

No, she said. Just as—gosh, how should I put this? I guess you could say they gave them to me as symbols.

Ah, he said.

But as you can see, she said, the gesture became commonplace.

He nodded and said, Uh-huh. Then he asked, But who *are* all these people? I mean, taking the time to sew up quilts and then just give the things away?

The woman folded her arms and sighed wearily, tried, he was sure, by his stupidity.

Mostly women, she answered.

I see.

Come to think of it, she said, they were *all* women. Either just before or just after I'd read, a woman would come up to the podium and maybe make a small speech, then usually hand me a quilt.

As a symbol, Bill said.

Uh-huh.

Bill didn't like that it was happening again: learning from a college person that he, Bill, was more unlearned than he'd thought.

He said, Can I ask another question?

Sure.

What was being … you know, *stood* for?

The woman hugged herself and said, They'd explain that in their speeches. It depended on the quilt. Sometimes women in my audiences shared the same illness. Or maybe they were simply in the same book club. Sometimes they were all, you know, abused sexually by their fathers?

Shouldn't have asked, Bill thought.

But most of the quilts, she said, symbolized the same *general* thing. You know: women needing to take the bits of their hearts that still worked and pull together to become a community. A community that could provide them, you know, security like a quilt does.

Bill thought about these abused women as much as he could. He sensed he should confess his intentions.

And no men ever showed? he asked, out of curiosity.

Around here? the woman said.

No, he said, and his face grew warm, as if from a new fire. I meant at the universities, he said. Where you read your poems out loud. I meant no men ever showed up to give you a quilt?

Again her lips parted. Even outdoors, her face was really good.

Not that I recall, she said.

I guess the men all ran off, he said, after breaking the women's hearts.

She smiled as if Bill were an insolent toddler. I'm not sure, she said, that these women would say that. The women who heard my poetry would probably say the men ran off after abusing or harassing or discriminating against them—you know, that the patriarchy didn't allow them equality.

I understand, Bill said, though he just then realized the word patriarchy might not have come from the word patriot.

Yes, it was sad, the woman said. Their complaints were more or less standard.

Can I ask one more question? Bill said.

Why not?

Who did these women want to be equal to?

Who else? she said. *Men!*

Bill felt the skin just above his lips tighten slightly. He pointed at his chest and said, Like me?

She didn't answer. Then it was as if she'd just bitten into cold toast, the way she frowned.

Like me if I had more money, he said, and then, again as if maybe he'd blacked out momentarily, with her now gazing off at the national forest, he found himself chuckling at his own joke.

But she now, it seemed, had put on a very small smile, one that appeared to be either fake or real or maybe a little of both.

Anyway, you've had it up to here with these quilts, he said.

Correct, the woman said. And no garbage can could possibly contain them. I mean, look at all those things—the garbage people would go on strike.

You could put one in a can every week.

Yes, but how long it would take?

Two hundred weeks.

Which would be—let's see. Two hundred divided by fifty-two ....

And here, right where her mind tried long division, he stepped toward her to give it a go. This was his most successful move, stepping directly toward the woman to place his lips all but against hers, no tongue, no kissy noise, just one dumb mouth on what sometimes proved to be very soft lips, with one arm loosely enough around her to let her know she was free to walk off, though, baby, he'd rather she stay.

But this time, with this professor-poet lady, he'd stopped. He'd begun the stepping-toward, complete with the aiming of his lips, and his whole body had shut down, with their faces less than two feet apart.

Almost four years, she said, as if she hadn't noticed any of this.

That's a long time, he said.

Especially after the quilts start bothering you.

He wanted to grab her waist but kept still. You can't just ignore them? he asked.

No, she said. And I've tried. But, see, nearly every morning they're the first thing I think of. All those depressed women, all those *angry* women, all that goodwill they put into gathering together to sew while sharing their oral histories—as well as seeing to it that one of them actually came to hear me read and presented me with their work? I mean, to what *end*, really? Me up here alone on a mountain, unable to sleep under even *one* of these two hundred things? Because every time I've tried, I remember my ex-husband and get ticked off and feel more awake than I have all day?

Now, it seemed, she wanted to take Bill to bed—and for him to be aggressive in making that happen. Wasn't this how it always went? Right woman, right place, wrong time by maybe a minute?

I mean, what kind of end is *that*? she said. I mean, for me personally, what has all this sisterhood led to?

Bill was sure she wanted him to try his move again, but the skin just above his lips, all the more stiff, assured him he'd prove worthless to her.

I have no idea, he said, about sisterhoods.

Well, I just don't know, she said. About *anything*.

Bill himself would bet on one piece of advice: in situations like this, you were best off to forget about sex and instead focus on the supposed business at hand.

But to him, what he'd try to do now was worse than trying to get laid. Wasn't overcharging the most selfish thing?

I might, he finally said, as if thinking out loud. I might be able to fit some of those quilts in my truck bed.

But that, she said, would altogether require you make more than one trip.

And again he knew to keep silent.

Then all a guy needed to do was add:

Yes, it would, ma'am.

To take all of them, she muttered.

Then they both stood facing the shed but not completely. Nor were they really facing the woods. It was as if they'd teamed up to face nothing and everything.

But in that case you'd need me to pay you a lot more, she offered.

Yes, he said. In most cases I would.

Tell you what, she said. If there's no other—how shall we put this—*creative* solution you can think of, just go ahead and make the several trips, and I'll pay you whatever. In the meantime, as you take care of business, I'm going inside to try to nap. Like I said, sleep's been at a premium around here.

He nodded, wishing he could muster an erection. Was this how guys his age fell in love? She was walking into the house, leaving him unsure if she'd winked or kissed his cheek or touched his arm as she'd headed off, and this time he was sure he'd just blacked out momentarily—she'd had that effect on him.

Or maybe the quilts had? He was, he now realized, sizing up his job. The things did look handmade. And they were as colorful as screwed-over women were plentiful. He tried to yank one free, but it stayed. It was too bad he no longer kept his rifle in the truck. He could knock on her back door, which she'd again left slightly ajar, and she and he could take turns shooting. He guessed she hated guns but would find it fun, to let herself, for just this once, close an eye and pull a trigger. He, too, would shoot, mostly to demonstrate, but also maybe a few times for his own hell of it, and they could guess which quilts the bullets came to rest between.

Or if any had made it through.

They could part specific quilts to see who was right.

That, he thought, was his *creative* solution. But shooting wouldn't solve her problem, since a quilt struck by a bullet still existed, and these quilts would still exist in her shed.

Then again, he thought, a body could always burn them. Of course she wouldn't burn them, worried as she'd been about that fire. But she had used the word creative. That was her code, wasn't it, for *Just torch the damned things?*

And, yes, it was true the foothills were dry, but there were no red flag warnings—he'd have known if there were.

He was, he realized, now standing beside his truck, facing the bed, the smooth red can. Blacking out was the only way to explain this. Yes, another body might call his solution arson. Yes, a fire like that could burn a chunk of forest. Though what good was a man if he couldn't give an older woman help?

Plus if she says stop, he thought, I'll stop.

He was headed for her house now, the smooth red can in hand. No wildfire will go anywhere, he thought. Not from no aluminum shed. Still, with her worries in his mind, he walked a perimeter around her house, fairly in search of a hose. Burning, he thought, was always the best way. And her hose was coiled on a flagstone like a rattler, some expensive yellow watering-thingamajig screwed onto it. This would be so easy she could have done it herself—other than maybe she lacked the guts.

But guts I have plenty of, he thought. He would even say yes if she wanted unprotected sex. Of course she was still inside, trying to nap if he believed her, which meant probably watching him through the thin gap between her drapes.

He set down the hose, aimed it. Opened the smooth red can, shook it empty onto the quilts. He couldn't believe she hadn't run out to stop him. Was she rushing now to put on her robe? Women like her liked men who liked fire, he was sure. He took his time screwing the can closed. Took his time searching his pants pockets for a matchbook, as well as tearing off and readying the match, but then there it was, multicolored and thriving, his flame for her job, easing toward skin of his. He flung the match, missing the quilts on purpose. Why hadn't she come out? He didn't like risk when it meant acting alone. *Really*, he thought. Why wasn't she out? He didn't need to fuck her, or anyone. He just wanted to see her.

But no one phoned him for what anyone wanted. They phoned because they didn't want to do the things he did. He lit another match, stepped closer, manned up to place it on a soaked quilt. This match burned lazily, tempting him to move it, and then, as if intent upon making him shiver thoroughly, it all went up with a roar, the shed, for a moment, risen what looked to be two inches off her yard, like some kind of homemade rocket manufactured in part by all those abused and pissed-off women.

Thing *launched* itself, he thought. You gather enough quilts, you could send a body to Mars.

And it wasn't too long that he thought about Mars before it occurred to him to maybe go home. He was familiar with this feeling—it crept in every time. It was kind of like fear but odder than fear, more like a renewed curse that all the days he'd lived could, if some judge decided, be declared by experts as an awful waste of time.

But whether he'd ever be imprisoned or not, there would always be, in his mind, the woman who'd given him oral sex only to call him a pyromaniac. Three women had called him that, actually, but two had been strung out on meth. In any case he was now in his truck, closing the door quietly. Why was he ashamed? Was this why he burned things, to have an excuse to run? Was he really twelve-point-buck-scared of love, like the woman who'd given him oral sex had said? For now, he just needed to keep backing out of this driveway by avoiding the drainage ditches beside it. That's what had prompted the prettier of the meth whores to screw him: the fact that he couldn't drive in reverse as well as most guys, which she'd believed meant he was nice.

Safe, he said out loud when the drainage ditches no longer threatened, the professor-lady's front door still shut. Black smoke tumbled skyward from the shed. Toxins, he thought. But he had it in drive now, the F-150. And there was no need to rush, since he could now probably talk to anyone smoothly. He could always talk more smoothly the more distant he grew. And the next day always meant someone else had lit the match: after all, sleep changed him like it did everyone else. And even before he was off this road the recycling professor lived on, his mind replayed his sweetest moments with women, as his mind often did briefly after he torched things. There were the very old women he'd hauled for, and there was the very young one he'd hauled for, and there were all those middle-aged ones he'd hauled for. The very young one had said she'd let him screw her any way he wanted, but he'd known, moments in, that it was far from ideal for anyone, man or woman, to be merely *allowed* to make love: it could approach ideal only if both parties wanted it, better still if they both felt need, which, for him, seemed possible with middle-aged women only.

Though this woman whose shed he'd just torched: she was *old*. And there he'd been, wanting to pleasure her. Did this mean he himself was older than he'd thought? Did fifty-eight truly mean the new thirty-eight, and was this idea of recycled youth why her frosted hair had excited him? Or was this—this *vibe* he felt for the professor-lady—more like him chancing upon the only soul he could be himself around, including the part that sometimes burned things?

In any case he now needed to see her. Needed to make sure she was alive and OK. What if she'd popped some pill to nap and hadn't heard the roar of the quilts?

He pulled over, flattened a baby white pine as he U-turned. Then he was speeding well above the limit toward her house, as if to shout to any nearby wardens, *Pull me over, you set-for-life pricks!*—and now here came her Prius, straight toward him, then veering to his left, and they passed each other without any waving or even making the quick eye contact strangers usually made on a mountain this high, and as he slowed down, still headed toward the smoke, he realized it wasn't his eyes that had darted away—the darting-away eyes had been hers—which meant that she, this professor-lady, was smart about the important things, such as who to love and who to talk payment with and how, altogether, the world worked. She was smart, very smart, like the doe now galloping on the road toward him was smart, wise about mating and danger and where to go when a body needed to hide.

Charity Gingerich

Beauty Is a Mountain We See When Driving Our Car

These days there is very little landscape,
just curve, curve, and—oh my, Christmas.

I am unprepared for any magic but that of mountain ranges,
blue and still and wordless, coming and going
in the fog. My heart is ringing its little bell
waiting for something greater than help, help, and echo.
Is there a language that contains another silence,
one shaped and deepened by the word? Elie Wiesel asked,
but of course he had a right to.

More and more, sadness needs its own special shelf.
But I am determined to keep mine prettily decorated:
see the snapshot of Mount St. Helen's? I slept once in its shadow.
We all thought it dead, and it showed us.

Charity Gingerich

Conflict Is the Only Way to Intimacy

There must be a cry before there can be an echo:
You understand *help* better than *blackberries*,
your body wired for thorns, poison, attack.
If we let your voice out in the rain, it would come back red tulips.

*

The woman has been very careful about collapsing her body,
the act of folding delicate, discreet.
She goes from a bridge with vines, and birds rummaging in trees,
to something you could pocket easily: a polished bone, a small cup.

Landscape in winter, imagining what is there, trying on joy—
the red maple drops her pocket handkerchiefs,
and because trees are too large to carry
from the countryside to the city, taking up watercolors is wise.

This familiarity with yellowish skies could be prophecy, or hope.

She wants a shed of light in these close green hills to have a potent fold/
    ripple effect,
and you, cupping your ear to catch each ringing note.

*

She is *yes* to you. Think about it. Put a finger in the wound
and think shape: land, maybe, or Blue Bunting: entry and exit.
This isn't metaphor, but longing, which is natural.

Charity Gingerich

After June

Outside, *form* happens: field, fritillary, sky.

In the garden, tiny melons sweat,
sweet moons under the sun.
I want to be still like that again
under my best dream tree, barefoot,
you up there at the window, humming.
Making sure of things. Even the sky
wore an apron of stars.

Survival only seems possible
from this distance: recognition
and acceptance the heart's two faces.

Now—

I am a stubborn fort
with bluebird sentinels.
The sea is a long way off.

Jacek M. Frączak

Yom Shoah Personalized: Five Drawings

In the summer of 1991, I was cleaning out the attic of my family's old farmhouse on the outskirts of Rawa Mazowiecka, a small town in central Poland. As I went about my business, I found an old envelope containing one hundred twenty photographic sheet negatives. The negatives, it turned out, had been found by my father in the abandoned military hospital on the day that Germans left Rawa Mazowiecka in January 1945. He was fifteen at the time. Since I am a photographer myself and dedicated to history, I printed them and, to my astonishment, found a personal photo-history of the war as seen through the eyes of a Wehrmacht soldier—the aggressor, the enemy, someone who had invaded my country, Poland, in order to wipe it off the face of the Earth, someone who brought ruin, suffering, death.

What surprised me was the banality of the narrative that was revealed to me. Here was a soldier stationed in Nazi-occupied Poland, who seemed to be recording a photo-journey of his summer vacation in some exotic land: full of banal scenes, the photographs took a souvenir-style approach to their subject matter. But there was something more that I could detect in them, something that hinted at the nature of evil—an evil that could invisibly poison an otherwise decent person, a law-abiding citizen, who perceives himself as moral and just.

I do not know the name of the photographer or where he was from, but he was often the main character of the photos. He was obviously a low-ranking soldier whose duties were primarily administrative. I have no idea if he ever fired at, much less killed, someone. But he was apparently fascinated by the devastation that the German Wehrmacht had visited upon the countryside. Through his camera lens, I could see his admiration over the scenes of burnt villages, bombed houses, and ruined factories.

He seemed to believe Hitler's message about the superiority of the Germanic race over the nations of Central and Eastern Europe—not to mention over the Jews, whom Nazis compared to parasites. Not being a combat soldier, the photographer seemed to miss and to some extent envy the militant glory of those powerful frontline Nazi soldiers who were responsible for the atrocities committed in Poland. (Keep in mind that Poland lost over 16 percent of its population in World War II: the next largest percentage was the Soviet Union, which lost a little less than 14 percent of its people. Germany lost less than 10 percent. If you're interested, the United States lost .32 percent of its population.)

Why do I say that the photographer was envious of the frontline soldiers? It's the way that he and his comrades posed for the camera, holding weapons like children "playing war," trying to make themselves look like the invincible, death-threatening Teutonic warriors who believed they deserved to be masters of the world.

Before the war, the photographer may have been a pharmacist, an accountant, or a carpenter; he may have been a loving husband, a doting father, a good German. But the Nazi ideology—just like the Communist ideology that blanketed the postwar Poland of my youth—bit into his soul. It made him enjoy the evil. It took him inside of itself and made him part of itself.

In August of 1991, I toured Poland with my American friend, Richard. I had invited him to vacation with me, and we traveled across the country together, visiting the Seaside, the Lake District, the High Tatra Mountains; we visited ancient towns and historical monuments. And we stopped to visit places of Nazi-organized genocide. My friend Richard is Jewish. One beautiful late afternoon we stopped at Treblinka, where the Nazis had installed one of their most horrific death camps. It's been estimated that over one million people were slaughtered there, of whom 800,000 were Jews. Statistics are faceless, mere numbers. But for my friend, the numbers mattered. More than 160 members of his father's family were gassed and then burned in the Treblinka crematories.

I had been well familiar with the history of World War II and of the Holocaust; it's hard not to be, when one is born a Pole only thirteen years after the end of the war. But on this occasion, as the afternoon turned to dusk, I was with someone for whom the Holocaust and Treblinka were a part of his family history. I will never forget that evening. As we wandered about the site talking, I could not help but contrast the tranquility of the warm summer evening and the serenely beautiful landscape with the horrors of this place and its past.

As an artist, I found inspiration in the photos that I had recently rediscovered and the stories that my friend told me of Treblinka. I found it important to tell the story of the banality of evil and of the ways that evil can infect almost anyone, if the conditions are ripe. On this last point, I am reminded of a short poem by Leonard Cohen entitled "All There Is to Know About Adolph Eichmann," in which Cohen lists Eichmann's basic attributes, revealing an ordinary man. Of course, Eichmann, for all of his ordinariness, orchestrated the Holocaust.

Through art, I also wanted to tell the story of total extermination; of being in the position of those who were denied dignity and life, all for an ideology.

In preparing to execute the series "Yom Shoah," I started collecting stories, personal anecdotes, and memories of those who had experienced the Holocaust. I talked to people, read books, watched movies. And then I set out to recreate the victims' experiences, using the Nazi photographs as an inset within a larger vista.

Each pen-and-ink drawing offers to expand the image that the German photographer captured, but while his camera showed a piece of the world as seen through the eyes of a conquerer, the larger drawing shows *what his victims saw* as they hid, or ran, or fell from gunfire.

I intended these "Yom Shoah" collages to be personal interpretations of the Holocaust experience, as recounted to me by my Jewish-American friend. But I should note that my own family suffered. Two of my grandfather's brothers died in Nazi concentration camps. Why? Because they were teachers. Poles, Hitler declared, should be kept at the lowest intellectual leve, so, during the Nazi occupation, only elementary education was allowed. And then my grandfather was himself killed by the Soviet Communists.

Finally, I wanted to add my voice to the debate about extremist ideologies that promise a better future for humankind—or, at least, for a select portion thereof, the so-called Aryan race for Nazi Germany and the proletariat of Soviet Communism. As an autopsy of these ideologies shows, they can expand and thrive—like a plague—in social and political environments where common and banal evil is allowed to take hold and reign over human minds and souls.

I executed nine drawings in 1993 and exhibited them together with the Wehrmacht soldier's photos in a gallery in Warsaw, Poland. Only recently have I been able to return to Poland and bring much of my original art back with me to the United States. (When I first left Poland, I left with little more than the suitcase in my hand.) In December 2012, I showed the exhibition in Springfield, Missouri. Now, some twenty years after their composing, I'm pleased to see five of my drawings from this set published for the first time.

Note: All drawings are ink-and-pen on watercolor paper combined with a sepia photo sheet printed on a transparency (diapositive), manually scratched and distorted. All were created in 1993.

Yom Shoah 1

Yom Shoah 6

Jacek M. Frączak

Yom Shoah 2

Yom Shoah 3

Yom Shoah 4

David Shumate

Lincoln

If it weren't for the photographs, you might think Aeschylus or Euripides had made him up. Or that he was one of those Biblical fellows tormented to the brink of what a soul can bear. But there he stands. Long black coat. Tall hat. Half a beard. Droopy eyes. Ears large enough to serve several men. Like the offspring of a midwife and a coroner. A tree impersonating a man. Alongside him, his generals seem daunted. Anxious for the day they too will grow into men. Then there's that odd mix of joy and sorrow etched across his face. As when a joke hits a little too close to home. Given all that's gone on—Gettysburg, Antietam, both Bull Runs, four long years of war, more than half a million dead, a wife moaning on the balconies, a child in the grave—given all that ... why hasn't his hair turned pure white?

David Shumate

Chumming Around
with Hemingway

He calls from Paris at one in the morning to tell me he just fished a marlin out of the Seine. He says Frenchmen were falling all over themselves to snap a photograph of him next to his catch. And though I know this is unlikely since he's been dead for half a century and marlin aren't freshwater fish, I don't dispute his account. After all, he's Hemingway. And I'm just some imaginary man. A few years back he showed up at my house dressed as a matador, swishing his cape about in front of me as if I were a bull. And when he asked what I thought of his getup, I said it suited him well. Though, in truth, he looked a little bit like an elf. He says one day we'll motorboat down to Havana and smoke Castro's best cigars. Then fly over to Kilimanjaro and sing a rhinoceros out of the bush. I let him go on and on like that. Ten tequilas into the night he claims he once made love to Marie Antoinette beneath the topiaries of Versailles. And though I know it's just another fib, I ask if he wouldn't mind jotting down a paragraph or two detailing the events of that moon-drenched August night.

David Shumate

The Executioner

It's not the lucrative profession it was back in the Dark Ages. So between executions these men supplement their incomes by singing opera or driving school buses or fishing for salmon. You see them on summer nights playing backgammon and later drunk and staggering home, leaning on the shoulder of a friend. No one gets anxious if a gardener starts acting eccentric and plants tulips all over town or if a tuba player loses his place in life and goes honking through the night. But when an executioner acts erratic, people take notice. They double the watch if he builds a bonfire in his back yard and spikes a stake into its center. If he hauls his axes and cleavers down to the hardware store to sharpen their blades, word spreads that danger is afoot. But it's time to call the professionals in if on some full moon you follow the echoes of hammers and saws down to the town square where he's hung a noose from the rafters of the gazebo and is cutting a trapdoor into its floor.

Lindsay Tigue

Pont-à-Mousson

Caleb's wife, Chelsea, doesn't miss Wisconsin at all. She tells him this before she leaves for the night, her black jeans tucked into black boots and her eyes rimmed in clumpy mascara. "Bah, oui," she says when Caleb asks if she'll be out late. She is starting to look French, act French, talk French. Her mouth even puckers into a pout when she speaks. It's the way the engineers at the foundry look when they show Caleb their pattern casts for manhole covers. He stares as their lips pinch around words.

"I'm going to Antoine's." Chelsea holds the door open, her hand clicks the bolt in and out, locked and unlocked, like a restless teen. Antoine is Chelsea's inappropriately young student friend. She met him on a bus. Chelsea pulls the door shut before Caleb responds. He listens to her pounding steps echo through the stairwell and decides: tonight, he will follow her.

It's Thursday and Caleb and Chelsea used to spend these evenings together, their "research night" they called it back home. They'd cook their favorite meal—baked chicken with cranberry salsa—and look through documents, share interesting facts, bits of their newest fascinations with each other. They'd always end up making out on the top of manila folders and interlibrary loans.

Chelsea hasn't been quite herself the past year, but during the last two weeks, Caleb's noticed, she has completely transformed. She no longer seems like the thirty-three-year-old history scholar, the composed academic with a sense of humor. It's as if she's reverted to some impossible version of herself. Back home, she was slowly finishing up her graduate studies; she kept changing her focus— passionately researching nineteenth-century religious movements one day and early American land management the next. Chelsea took a leave of absence last year and Caleb doubts whether she will ever return.

Caleb trails Chelsea down the stairwell and out into the courtyard. Outside, the air smells burnt and rusty with metallurgy byproducts. Caleb ticks off chemical waste in his head—carbon monoxide, hydrogen sulfide, sulfur dioxide, nitrous oxide, benzene. He turns away from the factory with its maze of rusted gray smokestacks and pipes. The sun is beginning to set over the low hills beyond the abbey, and Caleb follows Chelsea down a cobblestone sidewalk. When Caleb turns away from the foundry, it changes his view of the town— how lovely the old, peeling buildings can look, how quaint the wide arched bridge over the Moselle River.

About fifty feet ahead of him, Chelsea types French into her phone. He can tell by the way she pauses, poking at letters one by one as she walks. After she reaches the bridge, she stops, looks around. Caleb hides behind the faded stone wall of their building. The swans below her honk and she looks lovely there on the old bridge, her brown hair blowing in her face and sticking to her lip gloss.

"I can see you, Caleb." Chelsea parts her hair as it whips into her mouth. "But go ahead and follow me."

Caleb peeks around the cracked, stucco wall. "OK," he says. She continues on her way and, after she reaches the center of town, ducks into the market. He waits in the faded arcade across the street and sees her exit with a fresh baguette and a bottle of cheap merlot. She tears off a hunk of bread and plops it in her mouth. She throws a piece toward the fountain. "It's for you, Caleb," she says, as if he's a pigeon. She walks through the central plaza, past the arcade where he stands, and down a side street heading south.

At Saint-Gobain, the local factory, Caleb specializes in manhole covers. He is an archivist, studying their design and history. He usually works at the foundry in Neenah, Wisconsin, his hometown and manhole cover capital of America. Here in France, though, Pont-à-Mousson is the place. All over the country, roads contain cast-iron covers marked with the town's name.

Caleb hates living here. Their entire apartment is covered in baby blue linoleum tiles and the walls are pink and the windows finished with white lace curtains. They found housing at the last minute and, since Chelsea volunteers as an English assistant, they live inside the local high school in a vacant apartment adjacent to student dormers. Their unit sits above the cafeteria and overlooks a courtyard where students gather between classes. At all hours of the day, teenage snickers filter through walls and open windows. Caleb can hear the lip-smacking sound of kids greeting each other in the courtyard, their kiss-kiss hello. It makes him feel old and foreign. He's separate from everything out there.

Right after they arrived in France, Chelsea became enamored with the life of Père Jacques Marquette, the French Jesuit priest and explorer of North America. Marquette is also the namesake of the high school where they reside: Lycée Jacques Marquette. He spent a few years studying philosophy and teaching at a Jesuit institution once located on the premises. Also, as Chelsea says, Marquette is the namesake of towns and colleges throughout the Midwest. He established missions in the upper peninsula of Michigan, a few towns away from where she grew up.

Caleb brought Chelsea to France under the premise of his research. But, really, they came for her. At least that's what Caleb tells himself, that sometimes escaping can provide an answer. Nearly a year ago to the day, Chelsea was watching his sister's five-year-old son, Taylor, when the boy chased a runaway bicycle into the street, was hit by a silver Prius, and died. Whenever Chelsea talks about the incident— which is rarely—she describes colors. The silver car, the red bicycle, Taylor's green overalls, and the woman who ran out of her front door clutching a phone, the house behind her a deep shade of eggplant. Only once did Chelsea describe the paramedics hoisting Taylor's body, how she tried not to look at the pooling red blood in the street.

Caleb would never dream of bringing up the subject now. Lately all Chelsea wants to talk about is Marquette: where he walked, where he went, where he thought.

"I feel so connected to him," Chelsea told Caleb recently. She wore a black mesh top that formed spiderweb designs on her skin. "To Marquette." She'd stumbled in at two in the morning, her eyes watery, unable to focus. "We've crossed paths." She overlapped her arms in front of her face for emphasis.

"You high, Chels?"

"Marquette would have been much shorter than you." She stared out the window at the Moselle, black in the quiet night. "No, I don't actually know that." Her face crumpled like she was about to cry. "I made that up."

95

☾

At the top of the hill, Chelsea enters the Laundromat near the train station. Through the window, Caleb watches Antoine folding his too-tight black-sleeved T-shirts. Caleb sees Chelsea sitting in a chair watching Antoine thumb coins into the dryer. Caleb spies on her from outside a döner kebab restaurant next door.

At twenty years old, Antoine is thirteen years younger than Chelsea. He studies philosophy at the Nancy-Université and shares her interest in history and Jacques Marquette. Antoine's family owns a bakery near the church and he likes to loan Chelsea CDs of French chanteuses crooning melancholy love songs.

Through the window, Chelsea waves at Caleb, mimes eating, and points at the restaurant's sign. She wants him to bring her dinner. He orders the kebab and walks over to the Laundromat. Inside, the washing machines hum and the floor is dusty, littered with dryer lint. A sign on the wall says LESSIVE A MAIN INDERDIT. Hand washing forbidden.

"You're still following me," Chelsea says, before taking a bite of the kebab, a food item Caleb would never eat. The sight of the conical meat, like a sweating wasps' nest, turning under warmers all day in the window, repulses him. "I thought we were over that, the stalking, the protecting."

"Me, too," he says.

Chelsea finishes her kebab and Antoine shoots Caleb glares from of the corner of his eye. They never speak due to the supposed language barrier, though each understands enough. If they really tried, Caleb knows, they could converse. Antoine, however, hates him. "He thinks you're a philistine," Chelsea explained once and Caleb nodded. Most people didn't credit his love of manhole covers as an intellectual pursuit.

Caleb picks up a stray dryer sheet and holds it to his nose. He asks Chelsea about her plans for the night, where she is going, who she'll be with.

"I told you that already." Chelsea wipes a greasy hand on her jeans. "To Antoine's."

Caleb says maybe he'll just go with them and Chelsea nods and throws away the kebab wrapper and Antoine grabs his laundry basket and clothes. They all crawl into Antoine's blue Peugeot and the laundry gets stacked next to Caleb in the back seat. It smells like lavender in there, fresh and flowery, and Caleb knows he feels safer than he should as Antoine weaves around roundabouts, past the old church, before parking in front of the bakery.

A full two weeks ago, on a Thursday, Caleb began to worry about Chelsea when he came home from work and found her lying on the linoleum with her eyes closed. The early-evening sunlight filtered through the eyelet holes in the curtains and she looked peaceful there, a slight smile stretching across her face. Caleb asked what she was doing. He set a bag of groceries on the counter, pulled a chair from the table, and leaned over her.

"I'm imagining this place in the seventeenth century."

"What do you see?"

"Less of everything," she said, sitting up on her elbows, her eyes still locked on the ceiling. "Less people, buildings, trash."

"Plastic hasn't even been invented," Caleb said, wanting to put his hands on her arms.

Chelsea squinted her eyes in thought. "Not for hundreds of years." She nestled back down, wiggling her shoulder blades against the blue floor as if snuggling into covers. She shut her eyes. "The abbey down the street isn't here, just the Jesuit school, priests-in-training rushing by in robes, sheep on the nearby hill, the stone castle on Mousson a little less crumbled. It's quiet."

Caleb was reminded of Chelsea's behavior after the accident, when he began following her around Neenah. She would go to the site and, sometimes in the middle of the night, lie down in the street. She'd curl up close to where she'd seen the bloodstain, which slowly faded away in the rain and sun. Caleb began openly following her footsteps. He stood guard over her on the pavement and diverted any late-night cars around the scene. Chelsea didn't stop and neither did he, knowing she must not mind the company. They related silently this way for a while and it was as if Caleb was reading her diary, as if he had access to her thoughts. He felt close to her just watching, making sure she was OK.

When the accident happened, everyone expected Caleb to make a choice. It was his family or Chelsea, it could never be all of them. They could never fit all together again. When Caleb got an unexpected grant and the opportunity to go to France, he thought: this was their chance. He and Chelsea could get away from Neenah, away from his family, away from that awful mark on the street.

Antoine's family's apartment is warm and smells like sourdough, heated from the industrial ovens in the bakery below. Inside, his parents are in the midst of a dinner party—his mother passes a carafe of red wine to a woman draped in a purple scarf. "Bienvenue," she calls out and invites them to stay. Chelsea places her merlot and half-eaten bread on the counter.

The walls are painted gray and hung with geometric, abstract art. The dinner party, made up of three couples, sits at a wooden table under a large pendant light that looks like a dented globe. A man in tweed and silver-rimmed glasses pulls out a chair and beckons to Chelsea, as if he recognizes her. They strike up a conversation in French. Antoine goes around the room and kisses all the women on the cheek and then grabs the wine from a well-dressed man. He pours it for the table, hovering carefully over each glass. The empty bottles on the counter and the decibel level of laughter suggest everyone has been drinking for hours. Caleb pulls a chair over to the table and takes a sip of his wine. Antoine points at the small, thin woman with stringy dark hair seated across from him. "English," Antoine says as he sets the carafe next to a bowl of pears.

"Ah yes, I'm from Boston," the woman says. Her voice is high and abrasive; Caleb is sure he won't like her. "You don't speak French?"

Caleb tells her he knows a little, that he understands, but always feels people's impatience as he speaks. He can sense their need for him to cease talking, to finish. "My wife is better," he says. "She has a knack for languages." Caleb asks the woman what she's doing in France.

"Oh, I live here now. I married a Frenchman who was studying in the States." She points to the man engaged in conversation with Chelsea. The rest of the table seems caught up in a debate about the social exploits of the French president and his wife. Chelsea and the man lean toward each other and Caleb hears snatches of words: *Marquette, l'explorateur.*

"My wife is telling your husband about Jacques Marquette, it seems."

The woman nods. "It's a name I should know? It might sound familiar."

"The Jesuit priest who lived here." Caleb gestures toward the floor. "In France. In Pont-à-Mousson. And then founded missions in the Upper Peninsula of Michigan. And later, helped map the Mississippi." Caleb runs his hand through his hair, aware he is telling his wife's story. "Or part of it, anyway."

"And your wife. She studies him—this is part of her work?" The woman's English seems a little stilted, like someone unused to its daily practice.

"Something like that," Caleb says, staring at Chelsea who has her right hand perched over her wineglass, her fingers pressing around its opening. She laughs at a joke Caleb doesn't understand, some bit of French he can barely even hear.

A couple of days after Caleb found Chelsea on the linoleum, he found something else. He'd spent hours at the foundry organizing a file archive of manhole cover design plans. He got back late that evening and saw a torn scrap of paper on the table. It had been dipped in tea and scorched at the edges to look old, like a school history project. She'd written in English so, Caleb presumed, he could read it. The handwriting was Chelsea's, but a slanted, flourished version of it, as if she'd tried to make it look antique.

March 19, 1665, Jacques Marquette to the Superior General of the Order in Rome

> *The seventh year of teaching being completed, but the twenty-eighth of my life, with another round of studies before me, I approach Your Paternity … that [you] command me to set out for foreign nations, of which I have been thinking from early boyhood and the first light of reason, insomuch that I desired to go to them even before I knew about them ….*

Caleb read the note three times before moving. He kept the paper in his hand as he looked for Chelsea in the bedroom, the bathroom, the living room. Out the window, he saw her across the street, in front of the church. She ran her fingers over Gothic carvings in the stone. Caleb went out to her and guided her back inside, back through the courtyard past students making out on a bench, up the stairs and into their apartment.

"What is it? What's wrong?"

"I just wanted to see the church." She explained how the door was locked and so she examined the exterior, walked around feeling the ridges carved by armies of craftsmen, so many years ago.

"We could go on Sunday," Caleb said. "We could tour it." He didn't mention the letter. When he started following Chelsea through the streets of Neenah last year, they never spoke about it. Some things just happened quietly between them.

"I want to see the archways."

On Sunday, Caleb and Chelsea went to the 9 a.m. service at L'eglise Saint-Martin. Neither of them cared much for religion, but Caleb was secretly glad to attend. He found himself missing Wisconsin's zealous church culture a little, that community of so many other people believing in something. He liked to imagine those Christians in one place, under a vaulted ceiling, looking up. He found it strangely comforting. He'd expressed this to Chelsea once, before Taylor's death, before everything. "That's creepy, Caleb," she'd said.

At Saint-Martin, only a few people were gathering near a small space heater in the nave. There was no fruit punch, no Sunday School finger-painting on the walls, all of the things Caleb imagined church included. The cavernous stone building was freezing, even in the spring. Chelsea warmed her arms with her hands and walked around the perimeter. Once she had done a full loop back through the sacristy and around the side, she stopped in front of tiny risers full of prayer candles in glass jars. Caleb deposited a euro coin into a metal box and handed Chelsea a crisp candle. She lit it and placed it at the end of the first row.

She walked back toward the door and Caleb followed her. "The church construction began in the thirteenth century and finished in the fifteenth," she said to him, reading from a brochure. "I'm a terrible historian." She folded the pamphlet in her hands. "I should have known that."

"So Marquette would have come here?" Caleb pointed toward the ceiling.

Chelsea turned toward him, her face brightening at the reminder. "Yes."

They left before the service even began. They went and sat quietly at a café in Place Duroc. They sipped steamed milk and watched the pigeons land on the old, broken fountain. Caleb thought about the way Chelsea's face lit up at the thought of Marquette within those walls and he wanted to remember it, wanted to harness whatever it was that could create such a spark in her again.

At the dinner party, the thin-haired woman taps her fingers around the stem of her wineglass. "And what do you do?" she asks Caleb. She pulls her chair closer to the table.

"I work with manhole covers. I'm an archivist."

The woman smiles slowly. "And how does one archive manhole covers, exactly?"

"Photos, designs, that kind of thing."

The woman looks up, appears to be mulling this over in her mind. "Oh, wow," she says. "Tell my husband about this, too." She gets his attention and, in doing so, summons the eyes of everyone at the table.

Caleb takes a huge sip of wine, feeling the room's stare. He looks up, past Antoine's glare and toward the window outside. He tells the room how millions of Neenah manhole covers can be found across the U.S., how the Neenah Foundry began in 1872, how they started by making cast-iron plow blades, bean pots, and sleigh shoes. He tells them about Pont-à-Mousson covers, how Saint-Gobain started in 1856 after iron ore deposits were discovered at Marbache. He stresses the fact that manholes are access ways, he likes to use the phrase *subsurface conduits* when explaining them, but also tells them that maintenance hole is the new gender-neutral term. He tells them there's a maintenance hole in New York that's seventy stories deep, that they must be at least twenty-two inches in diameter. Caleb tells them Romans invented the underground sewer, that they were dug by hand and lined with brick, that some of their stone covers still cap holes in Jordan. Caleb can't stop once he's started. He tells them cover patterns are designed large because the iron shrinks while cooling. He tells them cast iron is iron that is melted then poured, that gray cast iron contains carbon and silicon, that these alloying agents give the metal its incredible strength.

"Ça suffit," Chelsea says from across the table. "Let someone else tell a story."

"Non, mais c'est très intéressant," the Boston woman's French husband says. One woman asks for a translation and the man recounts some of what Caleb has told them. He hears, "Accès sous terre," and the man dips his hand, as if demonstrating a pathway under the ground.

☾

Last Wednesday, a few days after the church visit, Caleb found another Marquette letter, this time taped to the bathroom mirror. Next to it, Chelsea had scrawled "xoxo" in lipstick.

> *August 4, 1667, Jacques Marquette, Cap de la Magdeleine, to Father Pupin, whom he knew from school in Pont-à-Mousson*
>
> *God has surely had pity on me. Since I have been in this country, I have felt no dislike whatever for it nor had the least thought of wishing to be back in France. You know that I had no memory at all when I was there ....*

Caleb found the letter after returning home to eat lunch and check on Chelsea in the middle of the day. Caleb searched for his wife again in the empty apartment. He heard the sounds of the cafeteria below ring through the walls. For a moment, he got down on the floor and put his ear to the linoleum. He could smell the couscous and chicken from below and he listened for Chelsea's voice amidst the din of French language and forks beneath him.

After pulling himself up, he walked outside, kept searching. He found Chelsea standing huddled in a group of French teenage girls, all wearing black tights and smoking. Chelsea took drags of a cigarette slouched against the building.

"Vous avez un problème?" one girl asked Caleb, after he walked up to the group and stared for a little while. "Qui est le mec?" she asked Chelsea, wanting to know who he was.

"Mon mari," Chelsea said. Caleb understood the word for "husband." Chelsea laughed and the girls snickered, said something in French about bombs, or missiles. "They think you're cute," Chelsea said, giving his biceps a squeeze. "Let's go back upstairs." She threw her cigarette on the sidewalk and stubbed it into the mortared crack in the cobblestone.

Caleb followed her up the steps and when they reached the door, he asked her what was going on. "What am I supposed to do?" he asked. "What are you telling me?"

Chelsea ran her hand along Caleb's ear. "Do you know why Marquette is famous, why we remember him?"

Caleb said he did not.

"Because his maps and journals survived, didn't capsize in a canoe. Poor Louis Jolliet, he went on that trip down the Mississippi, too, you know. And so did some other explorers we don't remember at all." Chelsea walked over to the television and turned it on. They'd borrowed the set from the school, an older classroom model on an AV cart. A French version of *Who Wants to Be a Millionaire?* was playing and Chelsea sank into the futon to watch.

"So, you're not going to explain?" Caleb asked.

Chelsea crossed her arms over her chest, kept her eyes on the game show. She shook her head without looking at him. "I don't even know if I could."

Caleb waits for the room to stop looking at him. Chelsea nods at him like she used to at her department dinner parties, trying to reward his nervous attempts at social contribution, to signal that he did his part and could retreat back into silent observation. Caleb decides to excuse himself to the balcony. The group pours brandy made from local mirabelle plums. Antoine hands him a glass on the way out.

Caleb stays outside and watches, sipping from his brandy. As he looks on, everyone seems to be getting pretty drunk—the laughter sounds louder, the gestures loom larger. People have to yell for their voices to be heard above the ruckus. Caleb's fogged mind feels lighter than it has in weeks and he wishes Chelsea would join him outside. When he turns away from the party, his view looks out at Mousson, at the hill and medieval castle ruins that sit atop it. He and Chelsea hiked to the top when they first moved here. They shared bread and a hunk of cheese sitting in the grass, surrounded by the remnants of a fortress.

When he resumes watching the dinner guests, Chelsea looks up at him from the table. She is explaining something to Antoine and his parents and she makes a circle by forming her hands into two facing "C's." She then threads her fingers together, squeezing her hands into one big fist. She points to Caleb and all four of them consider him, as if they are waiting for him to speak.

After the note taped to the mirror, Caleb looked for Chelsea's Marquette letters, waited for the telltale teabags and the smell of burnt paper. Last night, a week after her last episode, Caleb came home late and discovered their bedroom transformed. Chelsea had

Xeroxed illustrations of Marquette and tacked them to the wall so that it looked like the inside of a young girl's locker, or a bedroom celebrity collage. They all showed Marquette in his Jesuit robes. One picture depicted him looking almost frightened in a floppy, wilted hat. Marquette held a cross in one hand, the chain slipped between his fingers. The photocopy had been shaded over with colored pencils, all greens and yellows in the background.

On their pillow sat another letter:

> *May 1674 from Marquette's unfinished journal of his final expedition to explore the Mississippi*
>
> *… they also said that the great river was very dangerous, when one does not know the difficult places; that it was full of horrible monsters, which devoured men and canoes together; that there was even a demon, who was heard from a great distance ….*

Caleb crumpled the sepia-stained document in his hands. He walked through the empty apartment and this time, knew Chelsea wasn't right outside. He called her name out the window and then took to the streets. First, he checked Antoine's, but Chelsea wasn't there; Antoine hadn't heard from her. Caleb then checked the local bar, but she wasn't there, either. "L'amèricaine?" he asked wherever he went and people knew what he meant, that he was looking for the American woman who was acting fifteen.

Finally, Caleb thought to go to the one nightclub in town, Le Swing. It was only 9:30 in the evening, but Chelsea was there beneath the flashing strobes, dancing to DJ mixes of American pop songs. She was surrounded by a group of teenage girls and boys from the lycée.

"Caleb!" she shrieked when he entered. "Voilà!" She spun in a circle waving her arms in the air. She stopped and turned to him. "We snuck in."

"Chelsea, I'm sure that wasn't necessary." Caleb looked around at the nearly empty dance floor. The bartender glared at him while drying a goblet-shaped glass. "You're thirty-three."

The teen boys stood around Caleb with their chests puffed up, as if ready to fight him at any moment. The girls' faces revealed a mixture of apathy and judgment. They all wore black, and dancing had pasted their sweaty hair in little frames around their young, flushed faces. Caleb took Chelsea by the shoulders. He guided her toward home.

☾

Chelsea finally walks out to the balcony where Caleb stands. She runs her hand through his hair and scratches his scalp. "Ça va?" she asks.

"Doesn't Marquette bother you?" Caleb pulls Chelsea's drooping sleeve over an exposed bra strap.

"What do you mean?"

"You know, the whole imperialism, missionary thing, the fact that he discovered land that was already occupied."

"Oh, that," she says and shakes the sleeve back down. "Sure it does." Chelsea grabs the cast-iron rail of the balcony. "I just like the obsession, the purpose. How he used it to justify his life."

"I don't follow."

"I like to think he doubted who he was." Chelsea pulls a scroll out of her pocket, another artifact she has aged in tea and fire. She removes a rubber hair tie and unrolls it for Caleb.

"This is his report card from 1658. I found it in one of the books I'm reading."

Caleb takes the paper from her. On it she has written Marquette's evaluations in character, ability, and temperament. She includes both the original Latin and the English translation:

> *Ingenium (General ability) Mediocris (Mediocre)*
> *Judicium (Judgment) Mediocris (Mediocre)*
> *Prudentia (Prudence) Mediocris (Mediocre)*
> *Complexio naturalte (Temperament) Melancolica (Melancholic)*

After a minute, Chelsea takes the report card back and folds it into tiny squares and puts it in her pocket. "It seems he was a lackluster scholar, too." She grabs Caleb's brandy and drinks from it. He lets her finish the glass.

Throughout the night, they continue to get good and drunk on the mirabelle. The noise in the apartment seems to get louder and louder. The three couples eventually leave and Antoine's parents go to sleep. Chelsea and Antoine camp out on the thin, uncomfortable couch in the living room. Antoine plays a documentary about restoring a seaside village in Brittany that Caleb has trouble following. Caleb sits on the floor and leans his back against an armchair. Antoine tucks his legs beneath himself next to Chelsea. He points to the screen where two men in khakis chip away at an ancient seawall with a hammer.

"She's not going to sleep with you," Caleb says. When he hears his voice out loud, it sounds surprisingly garbled and drunk.

"Excusez-moi?" Antoine says. "Excuse me?" he repeats in English, as if Caleb is too dim to translate.

"I said, she's not going to sleep with you."

Antoine looks disgusted. He leans over closer to where Caleb sits. "And you, monsieur. You were not invited to my soirée."

"Hm," Caleb says, cocking his head toward Antoine and making eye contact. "Well, you were not invited to my life." Caleb lies on the hardwood floor and puts his forehead on his hands. He turns over and looks up at the lofted ceiling. The artwork hangs at odd angles. "You don't know what it's been like. What Chelsea's been doing."

"I know," Antoine says. "Je le sais," he repeats. He goes down the hall and into another room. Caleb hears him rustle around, the sound of papers moving. Chelsea looks toward the door, her face blank, as if she's still watching a movie.

Antoine returns holding a purple shoebox that says *Cache Cache* in cursive. He sets it on the Lucite coffee table in front of Caleb. Caleb picks it up and looks inside. It is a diorama. In it, a small plastic figurine draped in a felt robe and a twist-tie belt bends near a tree. There is a disproportional duck near his feet. The man appears to be standing near a river where a cardboard canoe waits nearby. Around him are hot-glued trees of various sizes and kinds, including plastic palms. To the figurine's right, on the ground, there is a large black circle colored in with marker.

"What is this?" Caleb points to the dark smudge.

"Un grand …," Antoine stops, switches to English. "Hole," he says. "A great big hole." He says "big" like *beeeg*, stressing its size.

Caleb runs his palm over the tops of the mismatched trees. Chelsea's Marquette stands in this landscape, yanked out of history, pathetically tending a gigantic duck.

Caleb sighs. "Chelsea," he says. "This has got to stop." He looks up at her, but she turns away, not meeting his eyes.

"You see. I know," Antoine says. "Je la connais bien." He slaps his hand on the transparent table.

Chelsea stands and Caleb watches as her eyes fill. "No," she says and stands over Antoine. "You don't." She walks over to the counter

106

and grabs her bread and bottle of wine. Caleb is worried she might drop it, but she motions to him and he follows her out the door.

It is two in the morning and Caleb and Chelsea sit in Antoine's parking lot passing the wine back and forth. The merlot is warm and velvety in Caleb's mouth. Next to him, Chelsea takes the bottle and pours a little wine into a puddle near their feet. Caleb watches it trickle into the spaces between gravel. He grabs the bottle back and gulps more so he doesn't have to see it. He's gotten so good at ignoring everything outside of their life here—it's been all he and Chelsea pan-grilling chicken on their miniature French stove. He and Chelsea wrapped up in their individual research, poring through documents at the kitchen table, the students learning all around them and gossiping outside.

"My grant's almost up." The words seem to come involuntarily out of Caleb's mouth. "We can't stay here forever."

"We have savings." Chelsea digs her toe in the dusty parking lot. "There's no way I'll go back."

"I can only stay another month. I need to be with my family, my sister."

Chelsea nods, takes the wine bottle and guzzles more down. "I know what this means."

Once they've finished every last drop, they get up and begin to stumble back to the school. For a moment, Caleb can pretend they're nineteen again, stomping home from a college party. He wants to yell and laugh in the quiet streets as they once did in Wisconsin, back when they didn't care who they woke with their shouts. Back when everything wasn't ending and it was OK to celebrate a world they seemed to own.

Chelsea pulls a letter out of her trouser pocket. It is intricately folded like a passed note in biology class. Caleb puts the paper to his nose. It smells like Earl Grey.

"This one's not by Jacques," she says. "It's about him being exhumed and reburied a couple of years after his death. He was thirty-eight when he died of dysentery."

"I don't want to read it. I'm done." Caleb unfolds the note carefully and then crushes it in his fist, tosses it in front of them. It lands only a couple of feet away. Chelsea retrieves it. She flattens it against her thigh and then reads out loud. "What occurred at the Removal of the Bones of the late Father Marquette. They opened the grave, and uncovered the body; and, although the flesh and internal organs were all dried up, they found it entire, so that not even the skin was in any way injured."

"Stop." Caleb pulls Chelsea close him, sticks his nose into the crevice of her collarbone. His voice becomes muffled by her body. "Ça suffit," he says in his terrible accent.

"Of course, Caleb," she says. "I know."

Caleb envisions the next month passing much too quickly. All of the ways he and Chelsea might say good-bye pass through his mind. In his worst fear, Chelsea simply kisses his face like a Frenchwoman, a peck on each cheek to send him on his way.

Caleb and Chelsea start walking again and support each other's steps as they pass through the plaza in town. Before they get to the bridge, they go by Caleb's favorite manhole cover. The design is simple, standard—little dashes in opposite directions, Pont a Mousson in block caps, looping the top. Caleb prefers it because of its location, that it's like a stepping-stone before the river.

"There it is," he says. He points it out to Chelsea and she sits in the street. She yanks Caleb down so that he is on the other side of the cover, facing her. They clasp their hands together as if gathering near a table for prayer. They stay silent until Chelsea tears her baguette in two and hands a piece to Caleb.

In between bites, Caleb tells Chelsea about manhole covers in other parts of the world, how some covers in Bermuda and New Hampshire, of all places, are triangular. How during car races through cities, covers must be welded down. Caleb tells Chelsea about covers in China; he explains how a few years ago people kept stealing them. Somehow, they could be wrenched from the ground and sold for scrap. Caleb tells Chelsea how dangerous it was, how pedestrians would occasionally fall into these holes in the road. He describes how out of nowhere, people dropped into the ground.

"Can you imagine?" Caleb asks.

Chelsea nods, her eyes closed and her head tipped back. Caleb takes her hand and brings it up to his face, sees her chipping black nail polish, her mood rings on nearly every finger. Chelsea's skin seems to glow underneath the moon, and for a moment, she is someone different altogether, someone from another country, another time.

Caleb used to wish for a maintenance hole right beneath Chelsea's spot on the asphalt, that terrible place where she pretended to sleep.

He wished he could crawl up to her there and pull her under the world. He only wanted to keep her safe. Caleb liked to imagine the two of them on ladders in that tunnel, looking through pick holes in the grate. And even now, he likes to pretend that maybe they could tuck themselves below the earth, take a passageway right under the river, and stop at the church, tumble into the crypt. He pictures them curling up for the night at the base of the reclining stone figure of a thirteenth-century knight. He sees the two of them heading out in the morning, walking below the pavement outside their apartment, listening for cars rumbling overhead, for wheels rattling iron circles in the street.

Melanie McCabe

The Mail

Every day, at least one letter arrives with your name
on it, but more often, two or three. The stack begins
to spill across the teak, and the cats take to napping on

this island of white. I should call to tell you not
everyone knows you are gone. If you have posted
word somewhere, it may have gone astray. People

are out there, awaiting your reply. I believe you may
have won something; your broker seems anxious
to share options you have somehow been living

without. A lucky thing that I am here to save you
from missing anything critical to your conduct
of business in this world. I should call to notify you.

I should call to say the cats are keeping warm
all that demands your attention. And perhaps
to tell you that soon this house

that has received and held so much of what you need
to know will no longer be mine. That strangers
will find these missives meant for you—

will bear the burden for you that I have been
carrying for so long. No matter what we do
or whom we tell, there will be days ahead when

someone sends us messages we will not be here
to open. Asks a question we will never have
the chance to answer. Who knows now who might,

in some distant year, return to love us, with no
better envoy than the postal service to say we are still
waiting, to let them know where we have gone?

R. Elena Prieto

Skyview Lake, Fourth of July

If this were the ocean,
there would be krill—
luminous, wispy floss
between whale teeth,
microscopic waltz
snuffed finally in the belly,
like those fireflies cresting
the darkened hill.
The crowd spaces itself,
spreads blankets,
unwraps sandwiches.
Before this is over,
we'll see anemones in the sky,
first the flash, then the breeze-torn
curls of smoke. For one evening,
calm waters and pearly constellations
winking in our nets,
the broach of the moon
cool and silken in our hands.

D. Gilson

Jimmy makes good coffee and I could sustain a whole library with (love) poems just for him

I spilt the coffee on purpose
so you would have to clean
it up & I could talk
         to you a minute
longer
         & forgive me
but when I bite into this cookie
         you baked
it is so sweet like your hair
        which I take whole
fistfuls of & shove
        into my mouth,
or somewhere close, that
            deepest
part of me.
Regarding the tree outside:
        forgive me again
if you liked it, but
        I cut it down
so we could live
in a log cabin & yes
this is just the first step
        I know
but you look nice
      in that KISS T-shirt
      & I could not help myself.

Cherie Hunter Day

Flash to Bang

Friction generates a pulse in clouds. If your hair stands on end like a mad scientist in a horror film, move away from the canyon rim. Now is not the time for photos of friends and family. That jagged discharge in the distance is three times hotter than the surface of the sun. Count the seconds between lightning strike and thunder's answer, and divide by five for miles or three for kilometers. Forget the distance. You are alone in a field. Crouch as best you can on the balls of your feet, heels touching. Lean forward, head down, elbows snug to the body, and cover your ears with your hands. This will make you small.

Cherie Hunter Day

Reparations

To break his coonhound from stealing chickens, my father tied a dead hen around the dog's neck as if the weight alone would cure the addiction. And when that didn't work, the smell of rotten fowl would change the poor dog's appetite. It affected us far worse than the hound. Death stayed close and touched everything. The knot in the rope wouldn't come undone. I can still see the shame in the dog's eyes flickering as he looked around the yard at random sparrows.

Gabriel Welsch

Shouting the Names

Coming out of the barn, stepping onto the gravel, or to where the gravel should have been, Gretchen's foot slid on the ice sluice that had melted the day previous, to freeze in the night and heave against the wood bib framing the door, and she went down. Something popped in her knee, crunched in her ankle. Even once she had come to lie still, she could hear the crackling skitter of the chicken feed she spilled in her fall as it continued to roll down the slope toward the lower floor of the barn.

Soon afterward she heard goats, then the occasional cow. The chickens themselves were strangely quiet, even though they probably crowded at the end of the their run and pecked away at one another's tail feathers. The weather vane atop the barn croaked its hollow copper call as it moved with the little wind that morning. What she did not hear was a truck, a screen door pop, a barn door sliding, a footfall, a breath, anything of another person.

She tried to pull herself forward, but the only way she could move without searing pain was also uphill. It was icy enough that each inch of progress was forfeited the moment she wiggled to move again. She imagined that the crows alighting on the edge of the barn thought she looked like a giant thrashing orange fish. She thought then of what she wore—Bill's hunting coat, grabbed off the hook, the last coat in the line before the door, an effortless and accidental gesture for the quick trip to feed the chickens and grain the cows. Underneath, a nightshirt and sweatpants, her daughter's, with JUICY written over the ass.

She started to call, to yell, simply *help*, and as she expected, the only answers were the bleats of goats, low moans of cows, and chicken chatter. She kept on anyway. It felt good to yell. Each time she did, her throat stung with the cold air, her chest contracted, one shoulder twinged. (Maybe she'd hurt a shoulder, too. Not surprising.)

She let herself really yell, half-laughing, near weeping, hollering whatever came to mind, profanities, the names of her sisters and her daughter, the names she had secretly had for some of the cows, the name Bill had given the largest goat, the names that together, she knew, painted her life.

She yelled Bill's name, yelling every shade of it she could muster, until his name became several beats, a single syllable blossoming into song. She knew she yelled at nothing. He had left four days before, half-lit, beer bottles crashing to the floor, a cigarette burning a stain into the kitchen table. At this point, he would probably only answer to his name if it were uttered by someone wearing a badge.

Out of breath, chest heaving with effort, she whispered and rasped out the names of her parents, the names of teachers she could remember, starting out at first with favorites but then moving through the sequence, so as not to leave anyone out. Then the scoutmasters, first hers, then those of her brother's she could remember, and after that coaches, and after them babysitters she used to hire, the contractors who knew the farm, the men and women who had worked the counter at the feed store, the mechanic, her hairstylist, her obstetrician, the man who arranged her mother's funeral.

Then, her eyes closed, the pain now dull but omnipresent, she mouthed the names of the sons she never bore, the men who never grew under the hard hand of their father, the boys who never learned to hurt, who never would join the hordes of men on this Earth who knew so few words for pain.

Gravel pushed at her cheeks, ice turned to water against her legs as they stung and then felt nothing, and no names came to her for some time, until she heard her own, but not her own. A repetition, her own voice mouthing the name she had earned, until she saw before her, kneeling, her daughter, saying again and again, *Mom*, and shaking her. Her daughter said, *Are you OK?* And then, *I can get you to the hospital.* And then, later, in the car, the rush of warmth making Gretchen sick, her daughter said, *I think I found out where he went.*

She didn't care, then. Her knee and ankle burned and throbbed and swelled and she thought of the cows butting their heads against the still-closed door, smelling the grain and lowing, and she thought of the goats tearing at roots, and the ice sliding into mud sliding into ice, and the price an acre of land might bring.

Benjamin Vogt

Pinus, Acer, Salix

It wasn't until I moved to Minnesota from semi-arid Oklahoma that I noticed trees, really noticed them in the way I imagine a baby notices everything—each new object and sensation a raw, naked, core-deep experience; something that shutters then echoes, coursing through the body. Those first memories color our experiences of the same sensations later on, as well as who we become for the rest of our lives. In Minnesota, the earthy musk of spruce and pine stands, with their cushioned floors of dropped needles, were primeval. Stands of maple, ash, and paper birch provided sounds I'd never heard—I could discern an invisible force through the cloak of the canopy, knew something of breath, fear, ecstasy, forgiveness, all in one moment—there was singing and whispering, there was conversation, there was self-expression and unseen purpose as the trees creaked and bent, caught and released the sky. I would sit still beneath the pine trees near my first house in Minnesota for hours as needles fell and massive Canada geese scraped south just above the conical tips.

Later, at the fourth Minnesota house, I became the designated planter of the replacement maple Dad picked up in his SUV—this after we dismantled two forty-foot maples that fell into our swimming pool during a summer storm. I don't remember how I got the job, but I imagine that it went something like this: my parents were either disinterested in planting the tree, or tired and distracted by other, more pressing concerns, and I was next in line as the oldest child. But the tree needed to get planted, for the reasons of its roots baking in the sun and the sudden blinding sensation one got searching for the descending volleyball during the extended family's weekly match on Sundays. Someone suggested that if you just guess when it will arrive, and sort of flail your arm up in the general location where you projected the ball to land, you'd most likely hit it, though that's not a sound way to win a point.

So one evening I set out to plant an eight-foot-tall sugar maple. I'd never dug in a tree by myself before, but it seemed simply a matter of increasing the size of hole I dug for perennials when I worked with Mom in her garden. And so that's what I did. No one, including me, gave any thought to the maple after it was planted—I don't even remember watering it, let alone checking on its verticality. I went off to college and years passed. Then one day on the phone my mom mentioned how it was thriving, nearly fifteen feet tall and at least eight feet around. I must've done a good job, she said, as if it were a miracle. I think it was.

Shortly after we moved in to that house six years before, my mom made sure that we set about finding a place for a weeping willow. As a child, she remembers the refuge of her grandmother's house in Racine, how she and her siblings would often grab hold of the willow branches and swing like Tarzan, their toes grazing the lawn. Since this was our permanent home now, after years of moving from house to duplex to house to house to house, it was time to put down roots.

My dad and I, after conferring with Mom, quickly decide that the best place would be about twenty feet from the lakeshore on the right side of the lot. Here, at the bottom of the hill, the willow should get all the water its vigorous roots would need. In addition, there was a thin arc of sun in the broken canopy above, created by a gap between the mature maples on the hillside and the scrub brush and young paper birches nearer the shore.

I don't remember checking much on this tree, either, after my dad dug it in. We didn't often make it down to the lake, though once my parents talked about making a beach, or at least some sort of gathering area closer to the shore. But it was impractical—the hill was steep, the mosquitoes intense (not the best word: thick-as-pea-soup would be better), and often the sweet stench of rotting organic matter, sometimes fish, was overwhelming. The willow, I imagine in my mom's mind, would not have kids swinging from its branches or fond gazes exercised beneath its canopy, nor complete a wistful scene. It would, like my maple I'd plant many years later, be left to its own devices. This wasn't uncommon in how my family practiced parenting—distance, respect, solitude, let you find your own way without their telling you what you can and can't be.

When I came back for visits in college, and certainly later while in grad school, I made my circuit around the grounds with Mom. The willow would always be a few feet taller, a bit scraggly, though, as it reached for the ever-changing angles of sunlight, but certainly making its way to twenty feet and much more. Its trunk was thick and sturdy, and beneath it, in the shelter of much shade, laid two stones—markers for two of our family cats; why we didn't place the other two cats here is something I deeply regret to this day, instead of handing them over to the vet to be incinerated. I'd like to imagine, though, that the two that are there have infused the tree with something intangible—the sense of our family, the sense of their own individuality—and that they have nourished the tree's spirit and given it, perhaps, a personality of its own.

I can believe this, imagining the roots intertwined in the bones of Camby, the loving kitchen cat who wanted nothing more than occasional sunlight and a cheek rub while sleeping atop a barstool. Yet she was forced into the small confines of the kitchen and dinette by another cat, who, if Camby stepped one inch out of her place to eat or use the facilities, would tear into her like there was no tomorrow. Once, she had a deep wound in a back thigh, tender, damp with blood. She would eventually die of unrelated kidney failure at twelve, too young, but she has now become something that towers over the landscape and will for decades.

This sort of symbiosis isn't simply a sentimental metaphor—the community trees foster is astounding. Their roots tangle and fuse with each other, creating synapses where information is shared—warnings of fungal or pest attacks, for example, so the next tree down the line can prepare appropriate chemical defenses. Tree roots also rely on a barter system with certain fungi in the soil, like truffles: the fungi get sugar from photosynthesis, and the tree gets key nutrients like nitrogen only the fungi can gather. In old-growth forests there might be around 5,500 organisms sharing and bartering in just one cubic foot of soil at the surface, where the majority of the tree's feeder roots are.

Trees also show a certain amount of self-awareness and willpower. They grow in unlikely places, from cities, to deserts to cliffs; they take an unusual amount of punishment from humans, who misshape them and leave them exposed to all sorts of illnesses and disrepair. Much to the chagrin of foresters and logging companies, no one can predict how a tree will grow: its own genetic makeup, the amount of light, the soil, perhaps its own will—so many variables produce a unique specimen every time, one which is defined by the seemingly chaotic mathematics of fractals, like much in the natural world. Trees can show great responsiveness, as when a stand of conifers in the mountains of Germany were affected by suddenly large amounts of acid rain and fog; the trees—sensing the end—pulled up all of their energy reserves and produced an incredible amount of seed, seemingly hoping for a better future for their offspring. The Douglas-fir, native to the Pacific Northwest, requires fire to pop out its seed, stored in cones in the canopy for decades—the fire clears the forest of other trees, while the thickly-barked and fireproof fir bides its time to change the entire landscape forever.

The value we place on trees isn't simply aesthetic or nostalgic. Religions throughout history have imbued trees with divine presence, most believing trees were either the gateway to or residence of gods. Many believed trees were the homes of other magical creatures such as sprites, fairies, elves, and demons. Religions like Islam and Hinduism prescribe high reverence and respect for those who plant and protect the lives of trees. Once upon a time in Germany, if a person tore the bark off a tree, they'd have their navel removed, nailed to the tree, and be forced to walk around the trunk until their entrails covered the tree's wound.

But across the globe the oak is perhaps the most revered tree, most likely because of its long life and statuesque appearance. The oak is also commonly hit by lightning, either due its size or some other factor, such as the rough texture of its bark that helps lightning travel erratically around and into its trunk. The oak is a divining rod of sorts, a link to the heavens. If you are a male, you're 89 percent more likely to be touched by god, and 30 percent of you will be twenty to twenty-five years old—a perfect time to enter the priesthood.

As a kid, our suburban lot was peppered with many trees added in after construction: three blue spruce, two Black Hills spruce, a sugar maple, a serviceberry, two clump paper birch, two green ash, and a few smaller ornamentals. Though I'm sure these were planted as much for beauty as for privacy, one couldn't expect to live to see their full glory. However, if you look at pictures in the first year compared to when I'd visit in grad school fifteen years later, the blue spruce were engorged eight times over, the sugar maple quadrupled in height, the ash—my lord—the ash became kings overnight, it seemed, making thirty feet within a few years, then kept going. I remember summer afternoon water gun fights—I had quite the arsenal stored in two duffel bags. My plan was to never be without a weapon, so I'd strategically place smaller guns in the thick branches of those spruce, and when my big two-liter guns were empty and I was cornered, I simply had to make it to a spruce for a reprieve, lending me time to refill the rest of my supply. Later on, I became the official Christmas light decorator, willingly, but was never adept or overjoyed at taking them down, usually in January when the high was five degrees and the windchill minus twenty. To this day, I am certain strands of lights are entwined and embedded in the branches of several spruce, and figure the new owners, discovering such serendipity around Thanksgiving, have started a fire while trying to plug them in.

In all the ways that trees sustain us, serve as examples of how to live, both in actuality and metaphorically, we've still lost some primal understanding of how they connect us to ourselves and the world. Science shows that they are unique, adaptable, cooperative, individualistic, determined. Memories show us they are places of psychological refuge. August shows us they are places of comfort, cooling in their shade and perspiration, ultimately life giving in their oxygen release and carbon sequestration. Trees are an act of foresight, hope, faith—a legacy of life. Still, Michael Pollan laments,

> Who today can imagine a summer day in the next century, sitting in the shade of a maple planted in 1989? Not many, judging by what we choose to plant these days. Gardeners in this country once planted trees with the kind of enthusiasm we bring to the planting of perennials today. What tree planting we do usually consists of marooning a few small ornamental specimens in a sea of lawn.

I live in a housing development. I grew up in suburbia. It confounds me why my neighbors don't even go to a big-box hardware store or nursery and buy a thirty-dollar maple, bald cypress, or serviceberry. One tree, just one tree "marooned" in the landscape, would someday become the landscape.

Just think about the beauty, the power that tree will hold over those who will inhabit the house beneath it. It's incredible. Then extend beyond humans to think about the birds, insects, and animals who take refuge in it—who also bring us joy and wonder in themselves. And if we went slightly one step further, and planted native species of trees we already admire and value, we could do so much to the world we don't see, but that we intrinsically value to the core of our being; an oak supports over five hundred species of just moths and butterflies, willow and cherry 450, birch over four hundred, cottonwood and crabapple three hundred, pine, elm and maple well over two hundred. Forests move north at a rate up to thirty miles per decade, yet this isn't fast enough to outpace the warming climate for some. The lessons trees teach are infinite, and our children, our children's children, will be deprived of much. No. They will be given the opportunity to have incredible experiences that will burn in them a sense of deeper awareness and belonging.

The other day I noticed a spider carting around a moth it had caught on a maple. A few weeks ago, after breathing into a willow, I noticed a branch move, but it was a praying mantis. In the curls of peeling river birch bark, spiderlings were hatching from the fuzzy goo of their egg sac. Four hundred miles from here, on a long thin spit of a lake, a house stands not unlike many other houses. No one knows who planted the maple by the pool, or even that it was planted. Someone just now noticed, camouflaged in the canopy by the lake, the weeping branches of the willow. A child picks up one of two stones near the trunk and carries it over to a playhouse or fire pit her parents are building.

Carmen Váscones

Panoptico

The body in its holding cell. The plague within and about. Vigilance, as well. Who has built a wall between us? Who keeps you from the shadow of the other so as not to contaminate your day?

A garrison marches in your brain. Your hideout is bombarded. Your guard is dead. Who is tossing your body in the pit? The war has reached within you.

And you believe in peace. Now if you could you would be there. It stinks, that white banner growing from your brains scattered on the map of the world.

Translated from the Spanish by Alexis Levitin

Carmen Váscones

Resistance of the Flesh

The mother whipped the girl with the ecstasy of a true believer stabbing herself with needles to fulfill vows of chastity and test doubt. So it wouldn't all have been in vain.

One of them, the mother, had the soul of a butcher, her body an ambush of melancholy and pain bent to sex consummated in the horror of a childhood tortured by incomprehensible prohibitions.

The other, the child, cultivated in her flesh a silent resistance unto death of her ancestral blood. Each lash settling the score of a desperate vanished love; in the dream's interval, vengeance dissipating without an oracle. She hones her filial blade.

A scream sealed shut in the body's urn.

Noise is the seal of the world's solitude. Blindness gleams like a niche lit by candles in the middle of memory. A haughty pride like a smile buried in a tender image.

Any gaze between them: a buried hook.

The only words she said, always like an echo, "Ignorance is my knot and my salvation," seemed an enigma frozen on her lips.

A chimera of lust is sacrificed in the small body. Between the altars of her pubescent breasts and tears: the end of our kind. From the beginning of her flesh the sign of pain. Feelings would like to play with the sea. Memory cracks like dried earth. No water in the wellspring of her womb.

Mother and daughter lapping at the breast of the moon. Neither able to submit. And only one can break the circle of taboo. They look at each other as enemies.

They repeat together: "The word was unmade flesh."

Blows of war are heard. Voices overflow. "In the beginning was my mother and my father, who was also her father." There is no peace for the body, ever.

The cell flees the mother. Its motion leaves a slash of nothing folded in time.

Translated from the Spanish by Alexis Levitin

Carmen Váscones

Vault

The immense wave seems a perfect curve, a uterine cave. A thick shell, purple-black. The breakwaters retreat into nothingness. Solitude explodes.

I am beneath the house, now I am truly lost. I appear floating within a sealed box. I feel safe in this thing. No one can touch me in here. I inhale without difficulty. I am headed towards myself. I react. How long can I keep on breathing?

Asphyxia does not awaken me. I cannot move. Is there no way out?

The tsunami inside myself.

Translated from the Spanish by Alexis Levitin

Carmen Váscones

Mute

In my childhood where was I? The child does not wish to be remembered. Pain overwhelms memory. The mirror is mute. There was no time to give the ghost a chance to exist.

Cruelty is so real it doesn't let one imagine or scribble out the dream before it dissolves in a grimace.

What will the enemy be like?

Behind my image in the mirror is the face of the moon spreading its she-wolf jaws.

I do not return to the well. An eyelid shuts.

The sadist emerges and dons his hood to swing his ax without thinking. He shatters the mirror. What will happen now?

Where is the reflection? One is left out.

Or so it seems.

(Who would you be without a witness?)

Translated from the Spanish by Alexis Levitin

Joe Meno

Janice Goes Swimming

Before Janice got beaten, she was singing along with her headphones—was listening to Phil Collins, as her taste in music had been the same ever since seventh grade—brilliantly, irrefutably bad—something her younger, more attractive coworkers often teased her about. She was thirty-four and hopelessly out-of-date on most things. She had decided long ago it was too much work to try to be interesting.

Across the river there was the city, partially aglow, occluded by the stiffly falling snow; before her, there was the abandoned nighttime street, the flash of her Metro Card disappearing back into her purse, the face of her watch frowning the time, ten thirty-two. She skipped over a pile of slush, mouthing the words in time to the bad, bad music. When the first blow struck the right side of her face with its terrible, indisputable force, she did not know what was happening, only placed a hand to her cheek and felt that something was very wrong with her teeth. The back molars on the right side were alive now, throbbing, the pain glowing acutely from the side of her jaw right to the tip of her nose. And then she frowned, thinking of how she'd just been to the dentist a month before and had to get two fillings: but isn't that the way it goes? Now someone was shouting loudly in her face and this one particular thought—the one about her recent trip to the dentist, the ensuing trouble with her insurance—appeared and disappeared before she could make any other sense of it, like a fireworks show consisting of a singular sparkly explosion. All at once she caught sight of her attacker—a man with a white blur of a face, wearing a red, hooded sweatshirt—and then another blow came, this one a short snap to the right side of Janice's skull, and as her earphones went flying from her ears, and the i Pod came crashing to the cement, she

130

finally had some idea of what was happening. She was being mugged, or raped, or something much worse, something so troubling that people, even in this day and age, were too embarrassed to ever mention; it was something that would destroy her and all her future possibilities, which, prior to this moment, had not been all that much, actually. There was her small apartment and her job at the encyclopedia company and a cat she had never liked who took green shits everywhere. And secretly, hadn't she had always assumed something like this would happen, something awful but not this sort of thing exactly, not something so public, so out in the open, something where all her lousy mistakes were lying right there on display? And then she began to get angry, wondering how it was possible that she could be mugged, raped, violated right in the middle of the sidewalk, at ten o' clock at night, right in the shadow of the Manhattan Bridge, right in front of all these newly renovated buildings, with the whole world secretly watching, judging her part in this, seeing her flailing like some cliché, and being a cliché made the moment much, much worse, because she was a person, who had done all she could to avoid becoming a cliché. Then this thought was gone, too, because now there was the full impact of the sidewalk against her forehead as the man pushed her to the cement, holding her there, and she was on her side, though which side she did not know anymore, and then the man hit her again, this time in the right eye socket and a pinpoint of white light exploded throughout the front of her skull and she was unable to think clearly at all after that. The only thing that was real was the intense physical pain erupting along her chin and throughout her body. Here was a hand now, here was a foot atop her pelvis, here she was asking "Why? Why? Why?" screaming the word but unable to make the shape of it with her mouth because it was already swelling up and now she could see there were actually two attackers—the one in a red sweatshirt, the other with a darkish, frightened face—and the one in the red sweatshirt grabbed a handful of her hair and began punching her eye, then her nose, then her chin again. The other man—who seemed smaller and whose soft, gray, fearful eyes were the only thing remotely human about the incident—kept on trying to get her purse. But he was not very good at his job. She was not letting go of it. She did not know that she was fighting, holding onto the red purse strap with all her might, the man with the gray eyes shouting,

"Lady, let go of the fucking purse! Let go of the fucking purse already!" because the other one, with his violent, too- red sweatshirt was the only thing she could see. The one in the sweatshirt punched her in the nose once more, and growled, "Jesus, just give us the purse, lady," hoping to plead with her, but Janice had been raised in a household without much money, and it was beyond her will or understanding to simply cave in, to just let the purse go, so the three of them paused, out of breath, these three persons who, only moments before, did not actually exist for each other—as bad weather, separated by the expanse of both time and space, does not yet exist, though any number of troubling currents, despicable cloud patterns, dangerous atmospheric conditions may well already be in place, forcing all these unfortunate elements together—and so Janice laid there, her nose bleeding, and began blaming herself, which was something she was often in the habit of doing. She blamed herself for taking the F train, for turning down a ride from Roger, lame, lame Roger, the fifty-five year old, divorced fact-checker who smiled like a librarian, for wearing a flimsy winter coat instead of a sheet of tin, for being thirty-four and still single, for not being one of the girls who could laugh at everything, for not liking romantic comedies, for not trying to listen to music on the radio, for being the kind of person who enjoyed books more than real people, for disappointing her father and mother by leaving Ottawa, for not being more like her older sister Karen, the world's happiest dentist, for moving to a city she thought she had understood but clearly hadn't, for ever doubting there was a blind, vengeful God out there just waiting to remind us of His unforgiving ways, for forgetting about fear, for thinking she had ever outgrown the idea of fear, for not being afraid more often than this, for not being afraid all the time, for not living and breathing in a constant, tremulous cadenza of fear, for ever believing in something like the "goodness" of her fellow man, for thinking that just because she was smart and well-read that she would be exempt from tragedy. Worst, worst of all, she blamed herself for ever taking the job at the encyclopedia—which was the reason she had been walking down the street, alone, at ten-thirty at night—because it was obvious to her now that the encyclopedia, like all things remotely sophisticated, was dead, and not just dead, but mutilated, desecrated, buried, and now, unfondly remembered. Here was all the proof she ever needed. The Western world was going back to the cavemen. No one bought encyclopedias anymore. Everyone got their information from the television or the Internet, and the idea of working until two in the morning, writing and rewriting articles about things as unimportant as the Korean War or the habits of triggerfish—*Triggerfish are extraordinarily aggressive— even violent. Some species of triggerfish, like the titan, are also ciguatoxic and should not be eaten*—trying to make some ridiculous deadline, was, at this point, plainly the saddest endeavor Janice had ever been part of, and the reason what was happening to her was now happening. Because being smart was on the way out. Being smart meant nothing compared to being strong, or physically dominant, or downright brutal. This was how nature worked. This was how the world, for ages, had arranged itself. Hadn't Janice been paying attention? Now the little man with the gray eyes gave another tug on her knockoff purse—a Kate Spade, which everyone in the world knew was not what the label exclaimed, though probably her two assailants were not attacking her because of its label—and the rough one with the red sweatshirt dug his thumb into Janice's right eye and began to press as hard as he could. The pain was so excruciating, so momentarily beyond all rational understanding, that her senses went blank, and she began to feel an immediate sense of relief, of peace, knowing nothing, in the short term, would get any worse. Feeling so overcome, her fingers relaxed and the purse went flying, spilling out its contents like a downed airliner. And then she could hear them scurrying away, like rats, like *rats*, she thought, finding humor in this but not having any idea why, and the worst disappointment was in knowing that even after she got up off the ground, even after she called whoever she was supposed to call—the police, her father or mother, her ex-boyfriend Will, someone from work maybe—even after she hobbled home, dragged herself into the shower, and was huddled, hiding in her bed, this feeling of stupidity, of having not known better, for being so easily identified as a buffoon, as a weakling, as a foreigner, as a phony, as a mark, would persist. It would go on beating, in her chest like a second heart, day after day, week after week, month after month, on and on, persisting in every empty elevator, in every shadowy parking garage, in the shower, alone in her apartment—the feeling of having been violated so complete—that already she was thinking of herself this way, in the otherwise, in the past tense, of how she used to be. Now nothing would be surprising. Nothing would be uncomplicated or beautiful. Every dark corner would be an occasion for terror. She felt bad for herself suddenly, for having ever come up with this thought. The snow kept falling in its unconcerned pattern; a streetlight leered at her savagely. Obviously no one was coming to rescue her. Because stuff like this happened all the time and even the worst thing that had befallen her wasn't going to be impressive enough. Even in her tragedy, she was kind of average. Though this was not all Janice thought as she laid there, touching her roughed-up chin, it was enough, before a crying jag or the dismissive tone of the police or whatever it was that was going to happen finally came next.

But then nothing happened. Nothing happened because Janice did not tell anyone. Dragging her sore legs and stiff arms through the snow, she made her way back to her apartment, holding the cell phone in her hand but deciding not to call anybody; instead she simply laid on the bathroom floor, holding an opened bag of frozen raspberries to her worried chin. She ate a few as she sat there. Then the raspberries ended up spilling everywhere, leaving bright pink stains beside the sink and she was too discouraged to clean them up. She would later come to think of them as her own blood stains, which was uncharacteristically melodramatic.

All of which led her to Mexico. Over the past three years, she had accumulated more than two weeks of vacation time and, impending deadline or not, she was going to get the fuck out of the city for a couple days, because as it turned out, the city was actually a pretty awful place. It was just like the jungle but not as pretty. And the animals here weren't anything you'd ever want to study. So she decided to call her friend, Denise, a girl she had roomed with at Uni; Denise was now a real estate broker down in Mexico, selling leaky condos to baby boomers going through second and third middle-age crises. She owned a couple of buildings in Cancun, and another one in Playa del Carmen, which is where she spent her winters. Their conversation on the phone was brief: Janice did not tell Denise what had happened, only that she was thinking of coming for a short visit, was that all right? Of course. Janice would take a week and a half off of work. She would come to Playa del Carmen to silently recuperate, to lie in the blazing sun, with as little as fuss as possible. She would let the tropics burn what had happened out of her.

☾

Before she could talk herself out of it, she bought a round-trip plane ticket, told her boss she had a family emergency, and then called her parents back in Ottawa, leaving them a brief voicemail that said: *Getting out of the city for awhile. You can reach me at this number.* Surely her father, who was a retired postman—forever tinkering with a birdhouse in the garage—and her mother, a secretary who had never left the city she had been born in, would hear the message, hear the curtness of their daughter's tone, the confusion in her voice, and know something was wrong. But what could be done? They were committed worriers, anyway, those two. After that, Janice went about getting her locks changed and handed a new copy of the key to the building's cross-eyed super, asking him to please look in on the cat, knowing there was a slight chance—when she returned—that the cat would be dead. Anyway the cat had been an ex-boyfriend's and was always staring at her with these insistent, judgmental eyes, and also dropping green shit everywhere. It might be better for the both of them if the relationship were to end. On that note, she opened the small window closest to the fire escape, much wider than she normally would, hoping the cat would be gone when she got back. Secretly—something she would never tell a soul—she had begun to blame what had happened to her, the attack—and all her other miserable adventures so far—on the presence of the cat. It was a bully, always head-butting her, always forcing itself up against her palm to be scratched, just like the rest of the city.

On the flight to Cancun, Janice got sick. She drank three Bloody Marys in a too-quick succession and then asked for a fourth, but the stewardess, a motherly figure, embarrassed for the both of them, pretended to be busy.

The cab ride from the airport was not as short as Denise had promised, and because of this, and because she did not speak the language, Janice spent the entire hour in a soft, restless panic. But then there was the giant, pink stucco house Denise had described, and they were standing by a satin-colored pool and Denise looked both older—in her bleary green eyes—and slimmer—just about everything else—than Janice would have ever guessed. She was wearing a silver two-piece that Janice would have never worn, not even in her early twenties when everything was still where it was supposed to be, and Denise was kissing Janice on both cheeks like some television aristocrat. It was then, pressing her cheek to Janice's, that Denise first saw the bruises, the scrapes, the marks ranging like tiny mountains from her chin all the way around her face.

"Wait a minute. What happened to your face, Simp?" Denise asked, using the old nickname, the nickname that no one had ever really used, because Janice had told everyone how much she disliked it, and Janice stood there, glancing at the rippling pool, and sniffled a little, unsure if she had the imagination or wherewithal to try and lie. She found she didn't. She slipped the big sunglasses off, saw the honest horror and delight dancing in Denise's eyes, and decided to tell her the whole story.

Afterwards, the first thing Denise said was, "And they didn't try anything sexual with you? You can tell me. I've been through some pretty rough stuff myself."

"No. I guess I was kind of surprised they didn't."

Denise said, "Well, honey, they probably didn't get a good look at your face," a comment which Janice was forced to ponder the rest of the afternoon.

On that first day, they drank cold red wine with fruit until it was evening and then the sound of tropical birds was replaced by dance music, blaring from the all-inclusive resort a half a mile away. Everything felt a little more lush here, the sky seemed closer, even the stars, and they split avocados and kept drinking well into the morning. The morning here felt like the beginning, not the end to everything.

On the second day, they were supposed to go boating, but the sea was too rough, and so they went to a bar with a thatched roof on the beach and continued to get plastered. This afternoon Janice had several piña coladas, though Denise stuck with her cold red wine. Apparently *a cupo de vino rojo* was the only Spanish Denise had bothered to pick up.

On the third day, they went to a spa and got massages from squat Mayan women and then smoked a joint, lying in overly comfortable pool chairs. The grass was so good and the chairs were so plush that Janice had a hard time getting up, even though she knew her forehead was getting sunburned. Later, they did not go out to have dinner in town, as Janice had no interest in being seen, even by knotty-eyed tourists and bland foreigners. Her face still looked like the elephant man's. They made jokes about it, tried on different pairs of sunglasses, but her right eye was as swollen as a boxer's. She was still having bad dreams. She was waking up screaming a few times a night. Denise was drunk, so she hadn't noticed, but, all in all, Janice was still in pretty bad shape.

On the fourth day, they went to a family resort, scowled at some fat American children for a while, and then made lewd comments to the youngish dolphin trainers, who all happened to be ex-pat Germans. They fed some too-friendly dolphins and then started drinking again.

On the fifth, sixth, and seventh days, they slept in the sun, allowing themselves to get burnt from head to toe. Janice hoped all the bruises, the scabs, the marks of what had happened would be magically erased by an awful case of melanoma, but her chin, it still looked like raw hamburger.

On the eighth day, Denise said she felt awful for not showing her friend more of the city, or the ocean, or Mexico itself, and so they made a plan to travel south to Akumal, which Denise said was the best place to swim. It was also had great snorkeling. But then it rained all morning, and they had to postpone the trip, and so they sat indoors watching a variety of Mexican talk shows.

After the third or fourth talk show, Denise looked up and suddenly said, "I hate living down here. I do. It's turning me into a racist. And a man-hater. The men. The Americans, the Europeans. There's all something wrong with them. Either they're divorced, or been to prison, or are trying to run away from something. This guy, this one guy I was seeing, John, he had been in prison for six years. For selling cocaine. He said if we were serious about each other, we should both get tested. You know, like tested for AIDS. He was afraid he was going to give me something he picked up in prison. I said,

"What are you talking about?' And he said, he was pretty sure he had a couple STDs. You know. From fucking the other men."

"Yuck."

"Yuck doesn't even begin to cover it. These guys, all the people down here, it's like the island of misfit toys. All of them are broken in some pretty substantial way. Why else would they be here?"

"Well, what about you?" Janice asked. "Why are you here?"

"Why am I here? Because I smoke too much pot. I got other problems, too. I think I might be masochist. I think I get off on dating crummy people."

"Well, why don't you head back home? Or move to the States and start over?"

"Are you crazy?" Denise laughed. "So I can work myself to death? Or get killed by some nut who has forgotten to take his prescription? No, thanks. At least I can still get laid down here without worrying about getting blown up by a fucking terrorist. Here, if they rob you, they at least give you a ride home."

Janice wanted to argue but found herself silently nodding, not sure if what Denise was saying was remotely truthful.

Another day went by, then another, and finally it was her last full day in Mexico and Janice had not been to the ocean, had not even been swimming, had not kicked her feet in the waves or the sand, and so they decided if they were going to go to Akumal, it would have to be that afternoon. Janice agreed, though they both accidentally took a late-morning nap by the pool, and when the phone began ringing, Janice mistook it for her alarm clock back home. She immediately began yelling at the stupid cat for licking her face—not realizing the cat wasn't there for several seconds—and then she understood it was her own sweaty arm lying against her forehead.

The phone continued to ring. Denise answered it in a stupor, nearly falling out of her pool chair. It turned out it was Janice's sister, Karen, the gleeful dentist. Denise smiled at first, nodding, laughing an awkward little laugh, which sounded sort of like a necklace breaking, and then she passed the phone to Janice with a look that seemed overly empathetic. Something was wrong with Denise's face. Was that concern? Was that what it was? Janice took the phone and shrugged.

"Hello?"

"Hello? Janice?"

"Karen? Is everything OK? What's going on?"

"Yes and no."

"What? Why are you calling?"

"I'm OK. But Mom and Dad. There's been an accident."

"What's going on?"

"Daddy's … he's gone. And mom … she's in intensive care right now. They said it doesn't look good."

"What? What are you talking about?"

"Janice. You need to come home right now."

"No, you need to tell me what happened."

"I can't. It's…it's too horrible."

"Karen. Just tell me what happened."

"I can't."

This was always the way with Karen. If it meant Karen knowing, and Janice not knowing, Karen would string it out as long as possible.

"Are you going to tell me or what?" Janice asked, trying not to shout into the phone. "I want to know what happened. Just say it."

"No. Please."

"Karen! Tell me!"

"It's Daddy. He's dead. He…please don't make this any more difficult than it has to be," Karen murmured.

"Well, I just want to know what the fuck happened to my parents."

"Someone broke into the house. Daddy…he down went to see what the noise was and…they shot him."

"What?"

"They shot him. They killed him. I…they haven't released the body yet."

"What about Mom? What happened to her? Is she all right?"

"She must have went down after they shot him. She…she's not conscious, so nobody really knows. They beat her up pretty badly. Her head got cracked open. They must have hit her with a chair or something."

"What the fuck? What is this?"

"I know. I know."

"Is this really happening?" Janice asked.

Everything—the whole world—had shrunk to the size of a head of a pin.

"I'm so scared," Karen whispered. "I don't know what I should be doing. I'm sitting in their house right now and there's blood on the floor and I don't know what to do, Janice. Please. You got to come home."

"This is too much. This is just too much."

"I know. It's bad," was all Karen could say. "It's so fucking bad," and then Karen was crying harder than Janice had ever heard anybody cry before. And then Janice was crying, too, uncontrollably, and Denise was putting her thin arms around Janice's head, and Janice did not like the feeling of Denise's bikini top up against her face, the smell of the suntan lotion so overpowering, but she thought better than to try and fight it, and so she let herself be held.

There were no available flights out later that afternoon, and none to Ottawa that night, so Janice stuck with the ticket she had and bought a round trip from JFK to YOW airport in Ottawa for the following day. This left the whole of the rest of the day to consider the grotesque details of what had happened again and again. It was devastating. Janice sat in the guest room for a while, using up tissue after tissue, and then, when those ran out, she began wiping her nose on the guest pillow, because she did not want to bother Denise for any more. Also, she did not want Denise to see her in such a state. Under the thin sheets, she thought of her father, his rail-thin mustache, the sight of him in his postman's uniform, and all the crazy birdhouses he made. There was one that looked like the CN Tower in Toronto, and another that liked like Mount Rushmore, and another that he had made after September 11 that looked like the Twin Towers. There were the birdhouses and his plastic goggles and the serious look on his face hovering over the whirring table saw. There was the memory of her mother, in the front seat beside her father, and Karen in the back, the four of them, driving to Vancouver one summer to visit cousins, her mother's voice singing along with the radio, something by Gordon Lightfoot. Her mother's voice was a little too high, but so earnest. It didn't matter that it wasn't a great voice; she made up for it with feeling. And then her sister was singing, too, and then her father, and then Janice was, and the windows were open, and the air racing in, so she wasn't embarrassed of how bad everyone sounded. And now. Was her mother alive or dead? What would she look like? Would she ever hear her mom's voice again? Why had Janice thought that nothing bad could happen if she was out of the country? What sort of life was this anyway?

After about two hours of that, Denise knocked on the door and tried to give Janice a shot of whiskey but Janice couldn't stand the smell. So they smoked a joint and then lay in the guest bed for a while until Janice sat up and said she thought she'd like to go somewhere.

"What?" Denise asked. "Really?"

"I dunno. I don't want to just sit here. Let's just get out of here," Janice said.

"Where would you like to go?"

"I don't know. I just don't want to sit here. I can't do anything until I get to my parents' house tomorrow. And this ... I dunno."

"Well, did you still want to go to the beach?"

"I don't care. That's fine."

"Well, we could go to Akumal," Denise offered. "It's close enough," which Janice answered with a nod and a shrug.

The cab ride was a half-hour or so, and neither of them talked. The cab driver was listening to American gangsta rap. Finally, Denise asked him to change it. He nodded, glanced in the mirror, seemed to take in the mood of his passengers, and then put on a sun-damaged Bob Marley cassette. The tape played a little too slowly, Bob's voice coming out light and warbly, and the sound of it made Janice feel nauseous.

The beach itself was all white sand, glistening in sloping splendor, the sun hot but shaded by a passel of drifting clouds. Europeans were in too-tight black Speedos. Americans looked globular, pasty, like uncooked loaves of bread, in unflattering bathing suits that were obviously the wrong size. Janice sat on the beach and tried to ignore them, ignore everything, staring out at the ocean, but even the waves seemed a little garish. Nothing was still, everything was bright and moving. People were laughing, running back and forth. Nude children were pedaling on their backs making little tidal waves. There were snorkelers with purple and green masks, fins like prehistoric fish, stamping back and forth, upsetting the water. Janice blinked, trying to block it all out.

"Was this a bad idea?" Denise asked and Janice sighed, uncurling her legs.

"Maybe. So what? It doesn't really matter now anyway. At least here, I won't cry like a loon."

Denise seemed easily appeased by the answer and leaned her head back a little, watching two hairy Italian men in super-small swimsuits jog by. Denise followed them with her eyes, and then glanced back over.

"Do you want to talk? I mean, do you feel like talking?" she asked, though it was clear Denise was not very comfortable with the idea of discussing what was happening.

"No. Not really."

"You're just having an incredibly bad run of luck. I had a year like that, maybe like five or six years ago."

Janice nodded silently.

"Do you want to go swimming? Or maybe you just want to lie here?" Denise asked.

"I really don't know. My head, it's ... I can't really focus."

Janice stared out at the snorkelers for another moment, thinking of something, and then stood, swiping the sand from her knees.

"Where are you going?" Denise asked.

"I dunno. I think maybe I'm going to get a mask and fins."

"Really?" Denise seemed startled by the idea. "Do you want me to come with?"

Janice looked at her friend, saw Denise had no intention of getting wet, and said, "Nah. Don't worry about it. I'm just going to go .... I don't mind being alone."

Denise nodded, lowering her sunglasses, and then Janice was standing, squinting up at the sun, marching off towards the dive shop.

She got a mask, a snorkel, and a pair of fins. The snorkel tasted like sanitizer, and the thought of someone else's soft teeth on the black rubber was enough to keep her from using it. She left it with Denise and then, like some maimed, miserable, mythological creature, waddled off into the shining water.

She had been snorkeling before on Spring Break, back in her second year at Uni, but that was in Florida and there hadn't been much but people's weird ankles to look at. Here there was the blue-green turtle-grass, brilliant parrotfishes, soft green brain coral, wavering fan coral, iridescent tangs, fish like biplanes, fish like jets, fish like submarines. The water was so salty and ate at the scabs and divots on her face. It felt good, actually, the buoyancy, the waves ringing in her ears. Her chin began to burn a little but it was so lovely, it hardly mattered. There were supposed to be giant sea turtles but Janice didn't see any. She did come across a school of tiny silver fish that radiated like a single plate of armor. Bobbing beside the school was a barracuda as long as Janice, with its crocodile jaws and lone, unmoving eye. In a flash, the barracuda darted at the school of fish, and then a murky gray cloud appeared, and the barracuda was snapping at something, swallowing one of the small fish whole, the school moving on, streaming this way, then that, content with its meager loss. She watched them for a moment more and then paddled on. The water was colder the deeper you dove. She plunged headfirst, blowing out a steady stream of bubbles. Before her, maybe four or five meters away, there was a line of bright blue and red cuttlefish—at least she thought they were cuttlefish or maybe some other kind of squid—small, torpedo-like, their tentacles raised above them, their gelatinous fins undulating like sails. There were five of them, and then ten, and turning in the water, holding the mask tight to her face, Janice realized, there were more than that, fifteen or twenty, all in a row, like a procession of some kind, each a half-meter apart, extending out to sea like a vibrant chain. What could this be? What could this mean? Each of the little squids had a single tentacle raised, almost like an elephant's trunk, in some measure maybe meant to be defensive, but even this was unclear. Probably they were all just braving the current together, as the waves here were pretty strong, and Janice could feel herself being knocked about, the water drawing her back to shore. But she kept kicking, diving down, floating beside the strange formation of squids, watching them fluttering in place. Had she begun crying then? She could not remember. This was the time she would think of later—the little squids in their endless array, arms raised together—as the moment she knew everything would go on, the same as it had before, because this is how the world was, as it had always been. Nothing had changed. It had always been violent. It had always been a rough place for the timid and the small. Now there was the implacable ocean, and the rocks, the undulating coral branches, the fish darting everywhere like individual, unspoken thoughts, there were all these tiny creatures fleeing, hiding, dividing into the dark, the larger ones chasing the smaller ones, eating them up. Everything was the same. Though her father was dead, and her mother was lying in some uncomfortable hospital bed, it didn't alter the course of anything. She could face it or not face it, but nothing was going to change. How could she go back to that awful city now, back to that awful apartment, back to that awful cat, back where everything was always meant as a threat? How could she face her sister, her mother, what had happened to her dad? She did not know. She bobbed in the water and pretended to be dead. A foamy wave rushed over her head; a boat sounded past. She drifted there, continuing to watch the squids, her arms and legs dangling loosely. And then, after some time, the squids began to flash and glow, their torpedo shapes pulsing with speckles and spots of radiant purple. In the face of Janice's agitated shadow, they had begun changing colors. It meant something. It had to. But Janice wasn't sure what. She leaned her masked face in. These small creatures, in their foreknowledge, buffeted back and forth by the current, continued to float, unmoving, mysteriously flashing at each other in random colors. For the moment, even this, even their terror, was beautiful. It was the terror of being alive, the same, anxious beauty of all living things, the fearful, glorious complaint of anything alive. Maybe this was all you could count on. Maybe this was all there was, this weirdly beautiful interlude, this panicked, joyful noise, this tiny, all-too-brief spectacle, moments before an impending disaster. Because who knew what was going to happen next? To anybody? Who knew? Maybe this was it. Maybe this, this singular, stupefying moment too small to ever mention to anybody, was all you could ever hope for. Was this some kind of an answer? How could anyone go on living like that? Could she? She did not know. She held her head under water, watching the animals strangely glow there for as long as she could. And then she was out of air, and was letting go, allowing herself to be carried back up, the world, the sky, opening up before her.

Jed Myers

Up from LA

The local madman seems to know
he's on the air. As we round the corner
he offers his listeners a review
of the local universe—we two,

producer and young star, he's sure,
arm in arm down the street to the car;
we'll cruise to the seaside hotel
to rehearse, in bed, our new thriller,

while our commentator finds an alcove
for himself and his cart of shreds,
covers himself with his coat,
wraps the night up with his guests ....

Psychosis—so sure of itself,
distilling its own cure of the dreads
with which it floods the senses. His
voice is definite—he *knows*

we're up from LA, on one of those
junkets of mutual self-display,
dressing and undressing together
as if the cosmos were our little theater,

all terrors at bay. On the street
where he sleeps, the gray asphalt
membrane bounces his announcements
into space, that treble sharpness

reflecting the hardness of the world.
How many listeners are out there?
I can imagine an immense audience.
He broadcasts bursts of certainty

out into a populous nowhere, facts—
the armies of Narcissus on Earth
in the Age of Mirrors, strolling in pairs
and catching their images in the glass.

Grant Clauser

Necessary Myths

There are certain nights
we pass through worrying
as wolves calling out
over the hills.

So what if Romulus
had put down the stone
and instead embraced
his brother?
Would our paths be
so different than now?

A farmer in Kansas,
to ease his stricken brother's pain,
puts a hand over his mouth
and holds it long enough
to watch the creases on his
brow soften with sleep.

And in the morning,
after collecting and washing the eggs
walks the mile to his neighbor
to borrow a suit.

It's hard, yes, to love
the stone in your shoe
when your whole life
is spent walking.

Jeff Alfier

Black Hawk Crash, Tal Afar, Iraq, 2006

The very name of the place you went down
sounds so remote you'd think it was history's
island of unreturned exiles, a plainsong
unbound from *Arabian Nights* where storied
winds sang twelve souls to sleep. Back
in our Ops Center on the Arab coast,
our colonel demanded of no one we knew,
Who sent them into that goddamned weather,
while we scanned the scratchy satellite shot
of your midnight wreckage, a sun-bleached
toy sunk to the bottom of a greening pool.

We set to work re-ciphering the secret codes
you'd carried aboard, not knowing
if our recovery teams would gather them,
or if they'd find other hands. As we worked,
a soldier at a Mosul firebase kept trying
to resurrect your voices, halted in the quiet
brutality of radio silence, as rain labored
against oily flames, aslant like streetlight
through a door thrown open in a distant city.

Neil Mathison

Dodd Narrows

July 25, 4:30 a.m., Ladysmith, British Columbia. The sky glows purple and pink, iridescent as the inside of an oyster shell. I've been awake since four, checking our sailboat's engine, turning on the GPS, booting up the laptop, opening the navigation program, reviewing the current tables, checking once again the hour of slack water, the distance to the narrows, our likely speed of advance. It's my catechism when afloat—rise early, prepare thoroughly. I'm half -awake. I could use a cup of coffee. But I enjoy the purposefulness of this predawn departure. My wife Susan and I often depart early, especially if we cruise unaccompanied by other boats. We like the stillness of the morning. We like watching the sun breast the horizon. We like the sense that we have become, by some sea magic, a first man and a first woman ushering in a first day. This morning, however, necessity demands an early departure. This morning we must reach Dodd Narrows by 7 a.m.

Last night, after my son John and Susan bedded down in their bunks, after my sister Charlotte's family bedded down aboard their sailboat, I laid waypoints into the computer: the first at Oven's Island, where we are anchored—our forty-two footer, *Allurea*, rafted alongside my sister's fifty-footer, *Integrity*—the second in Ladysmith Harbor, the third east of Coffin Point, a pair northwest up Stuart Channel, leaving Thetis Island and Pylades Island and DeCourcy Island to port, until the track reached the hook-shaped gap between Vancouver Island and Mudge Island that is Dodd Narrows. Square icons represent each waypoint. The track rubber -bands across the screen following the cursor like twine in a cat's cradle. The waypoints can be placed anywhere—mid-channel, on top of a reef, in the center of Vancouver Island: the software is indifferent to our fate. If I make a mistake, if I notice it, I can drag the waypoint to safer water. The track inflates and deflates as I correct it. The computer calculates a new heading, a new distance for each leg. I find the exercise pleasurable, like finger-painting or scribing figures in beach sand, although I miss the tactile joy of pre-computer piloting—the dry crispness of a paper chart, the cool steel of the divider in my hand, the sharp pencils, the stairstep movement of the parallel rule across the chart—from compass rose to track and back again.

This morning I've double-checked the waypoints. The laptop from its chart-table perch casts a lime-green light on the companionway ladder, ready to track our progress with its boat-shaped icon, ready to derive our position from the GPS, which in turn derives its position from the mandala of satellites above us.

Topside I prepare the boat. The deck is slick with dew. I work silently to avoid waking my sister's family. I check that lines run clear, that the dinghy painter is secure, that the air mattresses are deflated and lashed to the lifelines, that no child's plate or cup of milk was forgotten last night on the foredeck. The wail from the Ladysmith lumber whistle breaks the morning silence—the mill workers have beaten us awake. The current sings around *Allurea*'s stern. Susan stirs below decks. Soon, the aroma of coffee rises from the companionway. I turn on the lights: the rose-hued compass binnacle light, the red and green running lights, the white steaming light, the stern light that illuminates our ensign hanging limp on its staff. We're almost ready to depart. I glance at my watch. Three hours until slack.

The narrows lie twelve nautical miles north of our anchorage—at *Allurea*'s motoring speed, a two-and-a-half-hour transit. Charlotte and her husband DG plan to leave later. *Integrity* with her longer waterline and larger engine is, by the inflexible laws of hydrodynamics and horsepower, a faster boat. But, also, I prefer caution. We have a twenty-minute window to transit the narrows. If we are early, we wait a few minutes. If we are late, we wait six hours. Last night I warned DG to allow time for *Integrity*'s departure. Weighing an anchor can be an unpredictable evolution, but I suspect he considered my advice a brother-in-law's intrusion. The narrows are less than a nautical mile in length. Their northern exit is no more than a hundred feet wide. At full flood or full ebb, the current courses through the passage at speeds higher than nine knots, forming whitewater rapids and whirlpools and overfalls, drumming against the shore, and roaring like a mountain river's rapids. The weight of the Strait of Georgia, one hundred miles in length, fifteen miles in width, presses against the narrows. Only three other passes exist at the northeast periphery of the Gulf Islands—Gabriola, Porlier, and Active. None has a current as formidable as Dodd's.

I start the engine. The diesel rumbles below the cockpit sole. Will the sound wake *Integrity's* crew?

Susan comes topside. After a whispered good morning, she makes her way forward. I can just see her figure in the red glow of the port running light. She waits for my signal. We must be careful. If we take in the lines too soon, if the collapsible prop fails to pop open, if I miscalculate the current's strength, we will slide aft without steerageway and *Allurea's* bow may scrape *Integrity's* gel coat or our hulls may slam together or a dinghy painter may tangle in a prop. The throttle and gear lever rise on either side of the binnacle like a rabbit's ears. I press the gear lever forward. I signal Susan. I bump the throttle. We slip aft faster than I expect—the prop hasn't engaged; the current is stronger than I judged. Susan leans on *Integrity's* lifeline. She pushes the hulls apart. We veer aft, just missing *Integrity's* stern. An ungraceful departure. A reminder that boating is always an uncertain undertaking. But we are free, on our own, under way, on time. We motor out of the anchorage.

The sky is brighter now, glowing tangerine and crimson, backlighting the rough silhouette of the mountains thirty miles east on the British Columbia mainland. Dawn and dusk are my favorite time on the water. If the water is still—it is often still early—reflections double the world: the sky and the image of the sky, the islands and the image of the islands, the mountains and the image of the mountains. The wake behind us marks our course in pink, gold, and silver. But motoring into the sunrise requires a cautious watch. The sun is in our eyes. There are logs adrift: big Douglas fir loosed from mill rafts; windfalls borne seaward by inland rivers. I spot the dark profile of a sailboat heading north, bound for Dodd Narrows.

Susan takes the helm. I go below to check our progress. The green-boat icon on the laptop slowly follows the blue track of our course. All is well.

In the days before computer navigation, a navigator laid a track with pencil and straightedge, a process as obsolete for a navigator as a slide rule is obsolete for an engineer. The process is called "piloting" to differentiate it from the airier, more elite version of navigation known as "celestial." Piloting relies on compass bearings taken from at least three shore-based points, recorded in quick succession. The navigator plots the bearings on a chart. Where they intersect is a "fix," the vessel position at the time the bearings were taken. Both piloting and celestial rely on "dead reckoning," a presumption that, over the short period of time between fixes, a vessel's course will not significantly alter due to wind and current—a flawed assumption. The trick is to maintain a continuous plot, to mark the changes in speed and course, to fix one's position every hour. One never knows when the next fix may become impossible.

Twenty years ago, when I lived in San Diego, my brother and I set out on a voyage to Catalina Island. My boat then was a twenty-eight-foot sloop named *Margaritaville*. Catalina lay eighty miles north, about twenty miles west of Los Angeles. If we left before dinner, we would reach Avalon Harbor fourteen hours later, in time for breakfast. We cast off on a clear California afternoon. For a short period, maybe four or five hours, we would be out of sight of land. I busied myself with my piloting tools—parallel rules, dividers, the chart—taking a fix on the California coastline every hour or so for as long as we could see it. I planned to dead-reckon through the portion of the track when the coast lay below the horizon. My brother observed my piloting with bemused indifference, assuming, I suppose, that it was another obsession of his elder, overly cautious sibling. As Point Loma faded behind us, the wind dropped. We motored across a glassy Pacific. We watched dolphins leaping and the sun setting and the glow of the seaside communities—La Jolla, Carlsbad, Del Mar.

An hour after sunset, he called me on deck. The horizon was masked by fog. Nothing was visible beyond the glow of our running lights.

Do we turn back? Do we head for the coast?

If the fog lifts, I said, we'll see the Catalina light at 0500. If it doesn't, we'll enter the Avalon breakwater by 0700.

But my heartiness belied my interior doubts.

I returned below to recheck my navigation. There would be no "set" from our course because there was no wind or waves to push us off our track. The drift, the effect of the currents, would be modest, less than a knot. But had I compensated for compass error correctly? What about magnetic variation?

Variation is the natural drift of the earth's magnetic field. It is recorded on the chart, within the compass rose, stating the number of degrees change each year. Compass error, however, is unique to each boat and results from the distortion of the Earth's magnetic field by items onboard—electronics, stereo speakers, even an iron frying pan. And it varies with heading. A compass must be "swung" to calculate error and the result is a "compass card" that records the error for each ten degrees of heading. My compass had been swung, although some time ago, and before I bought the boat. I dug out the card, remembering the navigation mnemonic—*compass error/add east.*

I recalculated our heading based on error and variation. I plotted a new course to accommodate drift.

At midnight I relieved my brother at the helm. I steered into the darkness and fog, the compass my only guide. My thoughts were haunted. Was the compass card still accurate? Had my last fix been good? Was that a ship's horn in the darkness? Did I imagine lights? But I also thought how similar piloting was to life—the variability of the wind, the movement of the sea, the uncertainty of locating yourself, the constant, unpredictable change, and the vigilance required to hold your course.

At 0400 he relieved me. At 0445, he called me on deck. The fog had lifted. No light.

We peered into the darkness. Fifteen minutes later, just above the horizon, we saw a soft, intermittent strobe. I marked its bearing and timed its interval. It was the Catalina Light. At 0700, we motored inside the breakwater protecting the Avalon Basin.

For a few months, maybe for a year, my brother treated my piloting obsession with greater respect. *I was surprised,* he said later, *even impressed you found Catalina.* But he remained skeptical of my wisdom beyond navigation.

Susan calls from the cockpit helm. She still doesn't see *Integrity*. By now, even with her greater speed, *Integrity* ought to be underway, and she should be visible. I hail *Integrity* on the VHF radio. No answer. It's almost six o' clock. Ahead of us, we see the notch that is Dodd Narrows. The sunlight is brighter and flatter and silvers the water. We don sunglasses.

The Gulf Islands are familiar waters for Susan and me. We've sailed here for so many years that each trip evokes other trips and the layers of memories make every new voyage richer, like time-aged paint adds richness to a Vermeer or a Rembrandt. Once, only a few miles south of here, we watched a four-engine Catalina seaplane swoop down, scoop seawater into its cargo bay, and drop the water on a forest fire within our sight. Once, during a squall, I hugged the sandstone cliffs of Gabriola Island, just west of us, attempting to avoid lightning bolts. Once, swimming off the boat at DeCourcy Island— we are abreast DeCourcy now—John lost a front baby tooth. Susan caught the tooth just before John plunged over the side in a plume of spray. And once, having grown careless and forgetful, aboard an unfamiliar charter boat, I set out into a fog bank neglecting to lay a course or to compensate for the current or to check if the radar worked. We made our landfall three miles north of our objective, nearly running aground on a rock. In time, we groped through the fog, Susan on the bow, until we found the pass we'd originally sought.

Now, as we enter the funnel-shaped entrance to Dodd Narrows, the current is nearly slack but there is power in the green water. Several large logs slowly spin like a titan's toothpicks. I glance aft. Through the binoculars, I see *Integrity*'s navy-blue hull and the white wake that beards her bow. My brother-in-law is pushing her hard— perhaps as fast as nine knots. Even at this speed, she is thirty minutes behind us. She'll be late for slack.

For many years I've been the unofficial navigator of our family flotilla. I don't recall being asked to navigate. It fell to me. Or perhaps I assumed the part and maybe, even now, my sister and brother-in-law suffer my presumption. If my brother were here, if he didn't live in San Diego, if he joined our annual flotilla, my presumption wouldn't go unchallenged.

My dad welcomed my piloting, welcomed leaving the details to me, welcomed the chance to venture farther north than he would ever go on his own. We had reached the age where rivalry played no part in our relationship. But my brother and I haven't reached that age. We are similar and dissimilar. He is good with his hands—he can fix anything—where I will call a mechanic. But I am deliberate where my brother is spontaneous and his spontaneity is, in my view, sometimes careless. We share a passion for boats, a tendency to expound on our passion, and have little patience for those who ignore our advice. It is our similarities rather than our dissimilarities that cause us to grate.

At the onset of Dad's first round with heart disease, my brothers and sister decided to hold a sibling council. There was a question—I don't recall the question—regarding the course of Dad's convalescence. We gathered—my other brother, our spouses, and our children—at my sister's home. My San Diego brother flew up from San Diego.

I was reluctant to attend. I had quit my job shortly before Dad's illness and had spent hours with Dad, in the hospital, in his own bedroom, where we read together, recalled family adventures, and recounted our voyages. The time was our gift to each other. But the medical decisions I left to my mother. I was unwilling to navigate the specialists and surgeries and trade-offs his treatment required. Or, perhaps, I feared the course Dad's illness might take.

At our sibling council, my brother questioned Mother's decisions. Had Dad been discharged prematurely from the hospital? Was the hospice care adequate? Had Mother made the proper contingencies?

In the course of his interrogation, I made a remark. I don't remember what I said, although I'm certain it was sarcastic and inappropriate, born from anger at his questions, irritation at his criticism of Mother, and annoyance at his distance from our decisions about Dad's care. Now I realize he wanted to help, wanted to share the burden. His criticism was motivated by trying to help. But I didn't see this then. And maybe he didn't see the limits that restricted Mom's decisions, either.

To my shock, to everybody's shock, he leapt from his chair. He rushed across my sister's living room. He stood before me flexing his fingers, arms stiff, face white. And I knew, I knew as I gazed into his face, that my remark had pushed him beyond restraint, beyond deliberation, beyond any conscious course into uncharted rage, triggered by Dad's illness, but also triggered by other remarks made over the years, to other insults real and imagined. He swung his arm. My glasses flew from my face. I remember my glasses clattering against the wall. I remember the laughter of our children playing upstairs. I remember how my shock froze me just long enough for my other brother to wrap his arms around me so that I wouldn't strike back. I remember how that restraint humiliated me as much as my brother striking me had humiliated me.

Later, in an emotion-choked phone call, my brother told me that he hadn't intended to hit me.

In his words I heard embarrassment. I did not hear remorse.

I told him that I hadn't intended my remark to hurt him, that I was tired, that I was worried about Dad, that I'd had a glass or two of wine more than I should have.

But I wondered: was what I said really true?

Dad recovered from his first bout with heart disease. A year later, he died. By that time my brother and I had made our peace. It is an uneasy peace. We don't call each other as often as we once did and what we talk about never goes beyond sailing: our great reaches and runs; our favorite anchorages; our horror stories of failed alternators, blown-out spinnakers, leaking shaft seals, disastrous dockings; our close calls and our near-misses.

Despite these apparent catastrophes, sailing is a reflective pastime. During the long, eventless hours of a passage, your mind wanders; you have time to see connections between one thing and another, to sink below the surface of what you understand. But if you need to displace your anxieties, there are better sports—tennis, skiing, cycling—sports that demand attention, where decisions must be made fast and hard, where there is no time for reflection.

Now, however, entering Dodd Narrows, piloting demands attention. I see logs. Large logs. Fifty-footers. Logs jumbled everywhere in the channel. They turn in slow cartwheels. They form a dancing maze that no computer can navigate. I spin the helm, skating around each log. If we hit one, a glancing blow may do little damage. But in a few minutes, when the current begins to ebb, each log will become a battering ram, accelerated by the current and tide.

We clear the last, narrowest portion of Dodd Narrows. Ahead of us, all the way to the big pulp mill at Nanaimo, the channel is dotted with half-submerged logs, floating like alligators on the channel surface. A tow of big Douglas-fir has broken apart.

"Susan," I call. "Get on the radio. Warn Charlotte about the logs."

Susan pops up from the galley, spots the flotilla of logs, and dives to the radio.

Over the engine's drumming I can't quite hear Susan's radio transmission. But I hear Charlotte's static-filled response on the cockpit speakers.

"Hogs?" Charlotte says. "What hogs?"

"Logs!" Susan shouts. "Watch for logs!"

Silence.

Susan hails *Integrity* again.

No answer.

I slow down. We idle at the narrows exit. The current is already too fast for us to turn back. The center of the narrows surges with the water, its midpoint visibly higher than the shore. Whirlpools spin the logs faster. In less than fifteen minutes, the narrows have become a log-tossed Charybdis.

Ten minutes later *Integrity* rounds the hook, booming along, her hull skewing left and right like a tractor truck skidding down an icy highway. She plows past us, a hundred feet off our beam. My brother-in-law is at the helm staring straight ahead. I catch my breath. *Integrity* nearly hits a log. I call out. He doesn't hear me. Or if he heard me, he mistakes my warning for a greeting.

Later Charlotte will tell us that they had trouble raising the anchor, that they were worried they might not make the narrows by slack water, that they were going fast to make up for lost time, that the moment Susan called on the radio, *Integrity* struck a log slamming to a full stop, spilling the contents of galley lockers and bunks and closets.

Until a few months later, my brother-in-law never mentioned the logs in Dodd Narrows. But the next spring he asked if I would help bring *Integrity* through the Ballard Locks. "We're hauling her out," he said. "We need to see if there's damage from the log."

And that spring, when I proposed our itinerary for the next summer's cruise, up Georgia Strait, into Desolation Sound, through Surge Narrows and Hole in the Wall and maybe even transiting Yaculta Rapids, Charlotte's response was guarded. "I'm thinking about Dodd Narrows," she said.

Rise early, I told her. Lay out the track. Check the tide and current tables.

She remained skeptical. And I wondered then if someday, on a silent, early morning passage, when the sun gilds the water, if I might understand what lay below the surface of Charlotte skepticism or below my brother's anger or below my brother-in-law's silence and I wondered if might ever know when to help others navigate and when to refrain from helping.

But I suspect I'll probably never know.

What I do know is this: I will always depart early; I will always lay out my own track; Susan and I will always celebrate the illusion that we are a first man, first woman witnessing a first morning, and that we will always savor the dawning of a summer sailing day.

Conor Robin Madigan

Or on the Railroad

Janey Woods had an uncle who drank Sterno for five years and died of myocardial infarction. His sister had died in a similar way. He carried around her last bottle for a year and three or four months until he left it behind Smith Weston's bar and kept on walking until the Sterno stopped doing its job. He kept his sister's things all in a box—not even a box, just a three-sided cardboard holding device— in his room at the Y, but they ended up soggy to silt, behind Smith Weston's bar.

Janey's uncle, in attempting to contact God, once made a Sterno fire at the back of the Y and the flames crept the entire height of the building and left a scar of black soot still there as Janey smoked her momma's Capri cigarette in the dead-over-us sun of a noon day. What the newspaper said about the Sterno man, in so many words:

> Kim Woods, key cutter at the Gal Stop Service center for forty years, drank himself to death—on account of his bad heart—held a service revolver's handle attached to a child's telescope—found in alley behind Smith Weston's pointing to the sky—87, left behind daughter and two grandchildren.

Janey didn't know what to think of Sterno.

The locals had thought Kim wanted to die on account of his sister. It was a few minutes past noon and the kids at the church basement's day care made a collective sound, cheering their freedom. Sterno makes a child so drunk she swears her bones are receding inside her fingers. Sure, that's how it felt. Teeth. The one black man in my neighborhood walked his rescue dog by slowly and slower still, a pointy-nosed dog, both man and dog thin and slow. Jackets for the winter. Parking lots and gravel lots are good for getting drunk because when you get drunk, *this* drunk, you can mess around with anything on the ground and you don't care. Do not.

No one could die from this stuff. Too good, Janey said quietly through a loud face.

Damn attention-getters. Damn children. Making the hum of brightness on a sun-drenched noon. I knew one that died. In a coke grinder up in Altoona. My one uncle. They all did jobs like that, or on the railroad. Ate him up. Joe Pickins described it as the most quiet death he'd ever seen, Coke grinders being so loud. And he had seen Mark Cavinish slammed between two freight cars and tossed over a bridge. Janey's uncle did nothing with his life. They all found most of my one uncle's clothing on the sifter and only the shirt had blood on it. Must have been stripped clean naked. Weren't his shoes, neither.

Smith Weston found the dead Kim Woods next to the holster for his stargazer and a patch of really green grass and broken bottles thrown against the wall. Janey said all the tubes to his ticker shook and rattled and just gave their grip. Alley's no place to die, for Christ's sake, she said.

She lay on the gravel next to the black evidence of the Sterno fire and itched at her crotch with a tightened fist. The rest of the Sterno went to the ground. She hated on and on about it, throwing up in disgust and brightening right there before me in that sun. Why it all gotta come outta here, she said.

She said it all like that. Some here. Some there. Never a beginning thought to it. Just vagina. Why it all gotta come outta here, I said to laugh at her. Like pulling a car from an owl hole. Damn it. Dead people did not have to have babies. Dead people just kept drinking Sterno. Birthing that from here, she said. Remember holding the battery to your tongue until you just couldn't anymore, she said. But after there is a huge hole, not an owl hole. Jesus.

J. David Stevens

Capsicum

When he said early on that he worked in "food safety," she should have pressed further. Even now—the wedding planned—she wants answers he'll never give. "There must be better methods," she insists. "Liquid chromatography?"

But he says those tests lack a human touch. His job, people understand.

She's visited the lab only once, seen him belted to the chair, his chest and forehead a spiderweb of sensors. There's a microphone to capture any utterance, and after each session, he makes notes that are converted into numbers and plugged into the algorithm by Dr. Nakamura-Kleinman or Janine, the lab assistant. For the harsher tests, he says they do PET scans.

What she remembers is Janine—the vaguely medical frock, sensible haircut—dangling a pepper over his mouth. "Peruvian White Habanero," Janine announced, then slipped the chili past his lips until his teeth came together, his torso lashing the restraints as his jaw worked. An hour later, they were still collecting data.

"Who needs this information?" she demands.

But he shrugs. "Frozen-food makers. Restaurant chains. Lately a lot of organic start-ups."

His fridge is heavy on beer and dairy: yogurt, goat's milk, various things with sour cream. She says, "You don't even like hot dishes."

"They needed someone average. A higher tolerance would make me unfit."

On the phone, her sister preaches caution. "No man should burn so fast." And they both recall their father, who one day disappeared from their lives like a curl of smoke. The names echo in her head like a murderer's row: the Naga Viper, the Infinity, the Bhut Jolokia. She

160

wants to tell her sister that the Trinidad Scorpion is hotter than a police officer's Mace. She worries someday all will turn to ash.

But there are other things her sister—in her world of minivans and Topsiders—does not know. Like how, in his body, heat becomes sweetness. She tastes it when they kiss. She feels the nectar in her pores when their bodies linger together.

Or maybe her sister does know, which is why the line needs repeating, "No man should burn so fast." Maybe her sister can tell her secret desire, one she barely admits to herself: how someday the sweetness might become heat again. After a particularly torrid embrace, she'll look down to find their residue against the bed, some dying embers, a charcoal outline. She might even wonder why they ever needed bodies at all, her last flicker of thought as they converge in air, rising like flame.

Sarah Carson

After you wake

from the dream where the Giants play the Cubs, where a stray bat strikes the catcher's exposed thigh, and he says something that makes him famous, I am alone screaming at someone who is crying, and I am decidedly awake, not half-asleep. I slide my toes up to the edge of the light that escapes the crack between the kitchen door and hall, and I am certain that others out there in their own lights see me, see your footprints still wet in the hall, on the floor. It is September already, and we are still trying to negotiate for a summer. I give you two days in August for an entire July plus a camp song, plus a baseball game, plus a midsize trout that someone catches and lets go. I say it is seventy-two degrees and you insist it's ninety-five and there is no one around for miles except me and a boat that I've long learned how to steer out of the canal by the shapes of the branches that scrape out their names on sand, from beneath the bridge where one teenager scrawled "I love you" but did not sign his name.

Lori Brack

An Overture

Your nakedness against the white sink
fragile as a box of letters in a burning room.
You bend over the bowl of water, squint
into a foggy mirror giving back
smooth shapes of shoulders, neck,
face. You could be anyone. Your hands
on the keys, fingers full of sudden
beauty—once—I listened to fire
consume old pianos, ravishing their strings.
The world unturned, heaved up its ash
for us to sift, to save what remains,
our bodies holding here—just holding.

Lori Brack

Art History

Old man eats his Big Mac in the blue
McDonald's dining room. The frames
of his glasses are transparent. His feed cap
says Vermeer. What if other farmers somewhere
are wearing caps that say Rembrandt,
Caravaggio, Rubens? What if down at the co-op
they stand around the counter arguing color
and shadow instead of seed and till? The farmers
dream of dark lecture halls,
where they squint through dust floating
in a perfect cone of projector light,
straining to see just one curve
that tilts toward the baroque, a single
passage hinting at everything yet
to come, eyes hungry for the ripeness
they recognize as another kind of renaissance.

Gerry LaFemina

Emily Roebling's Rooster

—for Olivia

Mornings at her husband's bedside, she studied stress analysis and
calculated catenary curves then made the chicken soup she served
as he convalesced. Afternoons he awaited her return as she shuttled
between Bridge and apartment, he almost voyeuristic with his window
view and binoculars. Meanwhile, the workmen bricked the towers,
unspooled cable, while politicians and reporters bickered. Hours each
day she played courier, carrying the news, each snafu, the blueprint
changes. She relayed each case of caisson disease and, later, each fall
into the East River. And when the Bridge was complete, the *Brooklyn
Eagle* photographers came to see Mrs. Roebling, her carriage first to
cross– her husband left behind, still watching–a Brooklyn rooster on
her lap. That cockerel couldn't know it had been saved from the soup
kettle, from special sauce, from cockfights only to be lost to history
and to the pages of an unpublished picture book. It's a love story
between two horses, one from Manhattan and one a Brooklynite,
counting down till the bridge's completion. See: there's the rooster
in her arms. We can almost hear it crowing to let us know it was
with her that day, before the official opening, after all the dissent
had been silenced, when pigeons had already nested on new perches.
Gulls laughed as they always do, lurched downward toward the river,
then lifted themselves cloud-bound again. Young August Belmont,
seeing what could be done, began to dream of the fantastic, of trains
that run underground.

Renée K. Nicholson

In Sickness

The worst possible thing happened. It's what you most want to know and it is what I least want to tell you. Why is it that we must tell that silent, horrible thing? And how can I tell you, without being the object of pity? When you are the main character of your own story, the process of sifting through what you want to tell and what you're willing to tell is also followed by what is expected of you to tell. If I tell you I was a ballet dancer, it might pique your interest, but if I tell you that I was a dancer turned rheumatoid arthritis patient, there's something more there you want to read. I know it. I'm always told, "That's what you should write about."

As a dancer sidelined by rheumatoid arthritis, I often feel it is the RA, the uncontrollable disease that makes my story interesting, and that makes me feel cheap. It's a tough truth to consider that I'm just not that interesting to read about without the RA. Sure, I was never a famous dancer. Like many young girls, I gave a big chunk of my life to training, only to be suitable for pretty lowly work, to be a member of the corps. All I wanted was to dance. It didn't matter to me that I wasn't a star, so long as I could be a dancer. The word still holds promise for me, that fairy-tale creature my imagination conjured up in my youth. I tasted what it would be like to be her, and I'd be lying if I said I didn't enjoy telling those stories, even if they're ordinary. Lurking around the corner, through, is the RA. I feel like being diagnosed with RA gives my story something different, perhaps the star power my career lacked. Somehow, RA becomes more important. What's depressing is it happens to be the same thing I hate most of all about who I am. That's where the drama is, others assure me. But I know the truth. It's just an auto immune disease. It doesn't make me special; it just makes me sick.

More than anything, I don't want to be sick.

What makes me the most upset about writing *the RA story* is the idea that I might write about it and it will sound like I'm looking for pity. I'm surely not looking for anyone to feel sorry for me, to pull on anyone's heartstrings. In fact, I'm pretty sure that's part of why I don't like or want to write about the RA. I don't want to manufacture a version of me that dwells in the disease, mythologizes it, and gives it power through the written word.

Still, I think it is what you want to know.

Once, someone asked me to write about my sense of dread, as if I could feel the RA coming upon me. I can't recall who the person was, but the question of dread lingered like a thought bubble following me around. The problem about coming at it this way is that it's false. RA isn't about a building dread—it keeps a different timeline than that. It is a disease that often just shows up, and manifests itself in quick, devastating blowups. At least for me, things didn't build; from the time I first showed symptoms to my diagnosis was just a few short months—nothing, in terms of the span of a lifetime. It wasn't dread that I felt; rather, it was like when my computer automatically shuts down for reasons I can't explain. One day, it just happened and then I scrambled. My body just sort of broke down from the inside out. I played catch up, figuring out what to do because of this reboot. There wasn't much time for dread. I only reacted.

The first time I knew something was wrong, I felt it in my spine. I woke one morning to find that couldn't hold my body upright. Unable to work out the kinks through stretching, I went to a sports medicine specialist. He was a tall, athletic doctor in a crisp white lab coat. My appointment felt as normal as doctor's visits are—the usual procedures, like listening to my heart and checking my reflexes. It escalated; X-rays didn't show much of anything. My first ailment, my back, the doctor suspected the discomfort was caused by stress fractures. Not accustomed to major injuries, I was a little shocked. Even though I took good care of myself, this diagnosis wasn't beyond what I thought could be normal. I put my body through its paces six days a week, day-in, day-out dancing. The stress and strain, I thought, was catching up. This had happened to other dancers, and many returned after therapy and a short recovery period. I believed in my youth, and figured with some care I'd bounce back. My doctor agreed—a few weeks' rest and I should be feeling back to normal.

I knew there was more to these "injuries" when those few weeks passed and my back still hurt, and then my knees started to swelland other joints ached. It didn't seem right because I had been sitting out, resting. The results were frustrating. During a follow-up visit, the sports medicine specialist prescribed Daypro, an anti-inflammatory, and it helped for a time, and then, of course, it didn't. I'd swell up again. The more I sat in the white-walled offices that smelled of heavy-duty disinfectant, it dawned on me that whatever was going on with these so-called injuries, there was more to it. But I couldn't quite come to terms with the idea that my body wouldn't hold up. There was also no diagnosis to support any sense that this was long term.

When I thought I was ready to return, ballet classes fatigued me. I used to love the petit allegro, a string of light jumps together, bouncy and happy, but by that part of class I was lucky if I was still upright and moving. Sidelined, I watched other dancers rehearse ballets I thought I would be dancing. And while I watched as if I would soon be back in the ranks, I just physically couldn't get it together. Something was very wrong, and my body knew, put out the signals, before I could even begin to comprehend what was happening. I struggled through a few months of trying to dance before I knew—I just knew—these problems were much worse than the information I'd been getting. The sports medicine doctor told me that I might not have the endurance for dance. As if it could be that simple. At the time, this wasn't enough reason to abandon ballet. I just couldn't let myself think about what was happening, because the idea of not dancing felt unfathomable. What else could I do? I'd never thought of a future that didn't include dance. I found ways to make myself useful. I did light repairs to costumes, where threading a needle was harder than it had beenbefore. I'd chastise myself for acting ungrateful, for not sucking up my bad luck and waiting it out.

Still, at the end of the season, I didn't go back because everything hurt too much. I'd take a temporary break, I reasoned, and find a new doctor or work with a physical therapist and return stronger than ever. If there wasn't dread, there was doubt. I still didn't know exactly what was going on with my body, but I knew, deep down, something was wrong.

☾

Most times, when I make a change, the only thing I can do is focus on the change itself. Like a horse with blinders, I only see straight ahead, and maybe this blinkered self knows better than the rest of me what has to be done, how to keep myself from getting spooked. The focus is one what's to be done, not what's left behind. Did I know I was leaving performing? Maybe subconsciously I did know. What I figured out was not what to do with the rest of my life, but what to do the next Monday, the Monday after that, maybe the next month. Everything I did kept only the short-term view, leaving open what could be. Miracles sometimes happen. I told myself this even though I don't really believe it. In the meantime, I was happy to follow other paths because who knew, maybe one day I'd wake up feeling better and would slip back into my life of dance.

While my body continued to rage a silent, interior war on itself, I didn't talk about what was happening to me, not to my family or friends. I kept it locked up inside me, the same way I'm keeping you at arm's length. I even tried to keep myself at arm's length from the problems, trying to ignore the symptoms. I had to separate myself from the truth of my situation. Perhaps this was weak, a way of not facing the facts, but anything else would have been too devastating to me. I adapted to the new situation by never fully giving up on the old.

During this time I learned that I couldn't really be wholly unhappy as the slanted afternoon sunlight filtered through the persimmon and crimson leaves of trees and cast itself along the gray surface of Indiana limestone. The crisp autumn air made it easy to breathe, and walking outside between classes to the library became the way I remember college. To deal with the fact that I was no longer dancing, I literally shelved that old idea of being a dancer, leaving it in a remote dark corner of my psyche, like a box in the attic or basement gathering dust, full of cast-off clothes and knickknacks I wasn't ready to get rid of. Rather than dwell, I became preoccupied with other concerns. Then no one could accuse me of feeling sorry for myself—least of all, me. Pity parties just weren't—aren't—my thing.

College did open me up. I liked learning about new subjects— everything from freshman psych to Victorian lit, but nothing appealed to me so much as writing. I'd always kept journals, and so I happily lost myself in the world of the imagination, rather than focus on what was happening to my body. I wrote other lives, escaping the one I lived.

In school, to get by physically was literally just placing one foot in front of the other. Walking became something that felt like it could be managed. At this point, I could still hide the fact that my body didn't work quite right. I was stiff and sore, even though I wasn't working out all that much. Still, I shoved it out of mind, cracking open and literally getting lost in the books I read for classes. No one else could really see that I was losing control over my body. Not yet.

Maybe there is no escaping fate. That's RA—it's a fate, not a choice. Before I knew I was in the grip of a disease, before I knew its name and its ways, I discounted the symptoms. I wasn't dancing anymore, so I shouldn't feel lousy. But of course there were lousy days, many of them, and then, like a parting of the clouds, there were good days. As distraction, I made friends and went to parties and dated boys and tried to be what I thought was normal. Sometimes, when alone, I thought about ballet, missing the daily routine of class, but before the tears came, I would call a friend or rent a movie or open a book. My only cure was to do something, to take some small action that allowed me to not recognize the truth: I was not dancing. I still hoped for a return, of course. For a time, I lived in bliss between what could have been and what might be.

Only when my knees swelled so much that it was painful to walk, painful to sit, painful to lie down, did I seek any kind of help. When the swelling was something I couldn't hide, I had to do something. What I didn't know until one October night when I finally drove to a twenty-four-hour urgent care facility to get relief, was that I was going to be led by RA. I would have to try to understand that my body had been hard at work destroying itself, and that there wasn't a thing I could do about it until I asked for help. Even then, help would be imperfect. That night, the physician at the urgent care facility told me I needed to see a specialist. The swelling was bad and indicative of something else. I was given more anti-inflammatories and a referral to a rheumatologist, who would take my blood and run it thought the tests that would confirm that I tested positive for the rheumatoid factor, the surest way to diagnose the disease. I faced these doctors and my diagnosis alone.

☾

Gold salts, Daypro, Celebrex, Azulfidine, Enbrel. When you're a chronic disease patient, the list of past and present medications becomes a terrible little chemical parade. I need them and curse them. What bothers me about medication is the idea of being dependent. And despite the therapies I've tried through the years, my body still found ways to ravage me under the skin. My body had never been perfect. I'd worked hard to make it into a dancer's body. I remember once the mother of a boy I knew told me I had shapely legs. At the time, I blushed, especially at the word—shapely—which seemed to me so old fashioned. I was proud of the compliment, though. I no longer had those shapely legs, ones made of hard-earned toil, long, lithe muscle. My body hadn't always willingly conformed to a dancer's form, but I'd managed it and shaped myself through technique, good eating habits, Pilates, and hope. Now my body truly was an enemy, not something I might, through training and self-discipline, conquer. After my diagnosis, I accepted that I was sick, only insomuch as I might try to put up a defense against it. This second stage of decline happened slowly, a jag of bad days, limpy, swelly, achy days, followed by better ones, but never, ever days were I felt fully healthy. Over time, I just took on the daily hurting until maybe I didn't hurt so much or I didn't quite notice how pain affected anymore.

Or maybe I didn't want to notice. So much of how I have dealt with RA's blows has been to ignore what I've lost, how I continue to slip physically. Even when the injections changed from the old-fashioned gold salts to the new-fangled Enbrel, from something administered in the doctor's office to something I gave myself at home, I wanted to believe I could be better again. I wanted to believe that I would overcome it, that I wouldn't have to take anti-inflammatories daily to try to make my body behave. Maybe I even thought, beyond hope, that I could be a dancer again, to try to make my body be in service to beauty, that elusive ideal behind my desire to be a dancer.

Instead, RA continued attacking my healthy joints, despite all my efforts, literally eating away my cartilage, in some cases, until my joints were disfigured, and until all the healthy connective tissue was gone. I could only do what I was doing, but what happens when that's not enough? I had no answer save the cane I acquired to help me walk, to get around.

I have to wonder, too, is this really what you want to know, to read about? Think about it. If you read these series of events, that I went from not dancing, to not walking well, to needing a cane, to needing a walker, perhaps you feel better about yourself. Maybe you have problems in your life, but you have your health. You might feel better by feeling sorry for me. At least I never had to deal with that, you think. This is a pessimistic view, and it haunts me. I suppose I don't want you to think of me as a diseased person. No *poor girl whose dream was snatched away.* It feels cheap, and yet, here I am telling it. Perhaps I should think better of you. Perhaps I should consider that you want to see me come out OK, and that this is just where I battle my personal villain. That's the more hopeful view, I suppose. Perhaps too hopeful. What are we, together, trying to gain by this exercise? When we write our true stories, we're told there is a contract with you, the reader. The contract seems very one-sided. Tell us the whole truth, but make it worth our while. Don't make it up, but make it dramatic and poignant. Even better if you can work in the little-engine-that-could-myth—get knocked down and get back up. In the meantime, give us the gritty, terrible details. And here I am, putting it to paper. I have to admit, I'm a little ashamed. I promised myself not to use my RA to get attention, not to let it become a defining attribute of who I am. If I try to show you this side of me, this side I barely even let myself acknowledge, I wonder if there is a reward. In return for this confession, will you also accept my joy, small and personal as it is? Could you also love me in health?

The blue hanging placard in my car felt like a major defeat, because it physically branded me as a disabled person. No ballerina had been also physically handicapped as I now was. Alicia Alonso had danced even when she became legally blind, but her limbs still worked. I, however, ceased to work right. The placard arrived at a time when I required it. Most days, walking became slow and labored, and I needed to be closer to buildings and such just to function on a basic level. So, officially, I became handicapped. Maybe my ego couldn't take it, or maybe denial is just that strong, but I hated the whole idea of being handicapped and never fully appreciated that the placard and proximity were meant to help me. In my mind this was the antithesis of being a dancer, and even through everything I'd been through, there was that thread that refused to snap clean and allow me to think of myself as something else.

Of course, I didn't discuss it. If, when I was out with friends, they moved faster than I did, I just tried to catch up when I could, but I never asked them to slow down. I didn't ask for people to help me carry things or do things for me if I could help it. I hardly asked for help with opening bottles and jars, even though my wrists were thick with hot fluid and couldn't twist. Pride stood in the way of those requests. If I was tired, there was coffee, and if I hurt I felt it was my job to suck it up. No one would want to be around a person who was a constant pity party. More importantly, I wouldn't accept such behavior from myself. I certainly didn't pour out my conflicted feelings to anyone, either. If I didn't talk about it, maybe no one else would, and everyone, including me, could forget that I limped around, half useless. That's the best explanation I've got for why I just refused to acknowledge my steady decline. It's probably also a big part of the reason I've resisted writing about it.

I remember the day I realized I'd gone a decade as an RA patient. Other things, good things, during this time, had happened, too. I'd finished college and worked in marketing with some professional success. I'd gotten married. These are a few of things that made me feel like a pretty normal person. Ad hoc, as I lived with RA, I'd put together a different kind of life than the one I'd imagined. So, when a new coworker had asked me how long I'd had RA, and when I counted the years and figured out it was more than ten, I wanted to burst into tears. But I don't cry in front of people. Later, alone, the tears came. By the next day, I'd tucked the whole incident away. Time passed. My husband and I bought our first house and rescued a beagle, and I focused on these good things.

What persisted, though, was an old ache, and not a physical one. An auto immune disease makes you feel trapped by your own body. Nothing works like it should. I often thought about my youth, about studying to be a ballet dancer. Sometimes, in the kitchen, I'd try to do simple things, but I couldn't. RA had taken that from me. Forget *plié*. Forget ballet posture, erect, with stomach pulled in and shoulders down, the long, strong back. *Grand jété* —little bits of flying—a thing of your past. But if you complain about it, the disease wins. That's how I felt—pity was for the self-indulgent, not for me. Even if I wouldn't feel sorry for myself, I had to accept that living with RA was much different than the life I'd once hoped for. But forgetting was hard, especially when inside me there was that piece that just never wanted to forget the path I'd once been on. Once, I had danced and had loved it.

Truth is a tough teacher. Truth: you can't escape RA. Truth: you can't, at this point, do anything to prevent getting it. Researchers of the disease know there's a trigger for people predisposed towards it, but there's no test right now to say whether your genetic make-up makes you vulnerable or not, until you get it, and then, well, you're in it.

When I found myself in it, when time slipped by and slowly I lost more and more, I stayed in a kind of denial. That's a stage of grief, I'm told. Maybe I'm still in denial, hoping that by sheer force of will it would go away.

The awful truth: it doesn't go away.

Then there came the time when I made dancers on paper. It finally happened when I thought about applying to graduate school for writing, when I started to get excited about doing something with my life that gave me creative and personal expression. Sure, my limbs were anchored, but my mind, I hoped, could still reach and twist and soar. People choose to do MFA programs in creative writing for many reasons, and at the heart of my decision was the idea of recreating dance as word pictures, to keep it alive for me in some new way. I didn't want the dancer inside me to wither. I wasn't quite a writer—a part of me felt like battered old ballet dancer hiding out amongst writers. Still, I kept putting the language of movement on paper, its own satisfaction.

Writing about dance is difficult because dance resides so much in the body that it often resists words. I remembered, though, as I created characters to dance, the action verbs my beloved teacher, Mrs. Gooden, used: resist, stretch, release, bend, lift, gather, coil, reach, suspend. Dance lives through action verbs, which happen to also be the building blocks of good writing. Even though I was physically muted and stationary, the words cracked open again that world of movement. I wrote mostly fiction at first, and I found my characters aching for that beauty enabled through ballet that had been my ideal.

A common adage about writing is that it is a process of discovery. Perhaps all art is. For me, writing became the vehicle for rediscovering how much I had loved dancing, and how much I still loved it even though my physical being completely rejected it. Dance had made me as much as anything else, and I loved it completely, even as my body cast away all things physical, all the elements of a dancer's body. I could hope for better for those dancers I created in my imagination, who took form on paper in ink.

The more I wrote, the more my body declined. One really had nothing to do with the other, but the irony isn't lost on me. I've read about other dancers leaving ballet, and it's never quite like I did. My childhood idol, Gelsey Kirkland, wrote about her addiction to cocaine, and how her obsession with perfection through dance drove her to desperate conditions. She was once considered the greatest ballerina of her age, and to me, one of the most beautiful. A part of me wants to preserve her as that standard of beauty that made me want to be like her. The childlike glow that ballet ignited in me has never fully been tamped, and I often think that I've never shed my identity as a dancer, because even though my career was just a flicker, it lit a larger flame. A part of me will always be that young girl, searching for the promise of beauty only ballet seemed to offer, and when I lose that, I'll lose a big part of myself to a more cynical version.

I'm not wholly sure why I equate ballet and beauty, but I do, and so perhaps, too, I want to cling to the idea that I could be beautiful. It's such a common desire, I'm almost ashamed to admit it. Fact is, I'm not particularly pretty, but mismatched—pale skin and blue-gray eyes, but with dark hair. My head seems too big for my body, and my heart-shaped face has always looked pudgy, even when I was slender. I have a giant forehead that unfurls the way Antarctica does on a flat map—the great uninteresting plane of my face. My lower lip is bigger than the upper, giving me a crooked smile and perpetual pout. My skin rebels in little outbreaks of acne. The muscles in my legs, which used to be strong, are punchier, rounder than I'd like, and my torso is a little too long for the rest of my proportions. I have a butt, too much rump for a ballerina, and hips, but while I was dancing and thinner, I was flat-chested, and so I looked lopsided and a bit pear-shaped, which wasn't desirable, either.

My hands, though, used to be lovely—delicate with long fingers. Smooth, unwrinkled skin. I even had naturally pretty fingernails that looked as if I had them French manicured. My hands are a great casualty of RA, showing the effects of swelling and inner deterioration, a knobbier version with thick fingers and swollen knuckles. But once I had the hands of a ballerina, and even I liked how they looked.

☾

Imagine, once you had performed splits in midair. Now, sitting in a doctor's office chair, you're shown an X-ray that confirms that you no longer have any cartilage in your right knee. For years, you've hobbled around with the aid of cane, but now even that's not an option. You have two choices. You either have a total knee replacement, or you try to figure out a life getting around with a walker or wheelchair.

You are thirty-six years old.

One of the few times I've cried in public was that day in my rheumatologist's office. I guess it wasn't so public, but it wasn't alone. I hate that I broke down like, that but finally I couldn't keep my composure. My rheumatologist is a kind man, with a no-nonsense way about talking about RA. The choices were limited and I had to accept that. I already had, of course, because by this time, putting weight on my leg was more pain that I could hide, and relying on a cane was not enough. I could barely walk, but I did, perhaps by sheer willpower to get from one place to another.

Instead of telling me not to cry, my rheumatologist let the sobs flow, until there was a break, and then he brought me into his business office and he personally called the orthopedic surgeon he thought was the best in town. He took such a personal interest in making sure I was going to do this thing I didn't want to do with the best possible professional. I think he knew I'd already decided to have the knee-replacement surgery, but both my rheumatologist and the orthopedic gave me the option of calling back with a decision. I slept on it, but didn't toss or turn a bit. I knew I had to get the surgery, so first thing in the morning, I called and asked for the next available appointment. Once I made the decision, I was determined to get it done as soon as possible. No waiting around or mulling it over. Once again, I moved on quickly.

Though I was able to get in for surgery within a couple of weeks of determining I would need a knee replacement, I still needed a way to get around in the meantime, and so I found myself in a medical supply store, shopping for a walker. I wanted something basic, because I was hoping that I wouldn't need it all that much—just pre- and post-op. Strangely, this view betrayed optimism I hadn't dared to feel in a long time.

In the store with me were two elderly ladies. One was checking out a high-end walker, with wheels and hand brakes like a bike. The salesperson had tried talking me into a similar model, but I wanted the cheaper one, without wheels, without bells and whistles. Basic worked for me. It seemed weird to think of walkers as having bells and whistles, but they do. The other elderly lady in the store was buying a walker organizer—which is a fabric caddy, with various pockets, that fits over the bar across the front of the walker, so that, because both your hands are engaged with using the walker to move, you can keep things like keys and cell phones handy. The elderly lady suggested I also get a walker organizer. She showed me the "fancy" ones made of zebra-, cheetah-, and leopard-print fabrics.

I decided right there I would just use a backpack or pockets. It was too much for me to consider a cheetah-print walker organizer. Not only didn't it seem fashion-forward, as the salesperson reasoned, but I'd only accepted the need for the walker. I was not ready to give in to accessorizing, of making the apparatus some sad statement, not even when the salesperson asked if I might also like the see the giraffe print.

During the time before my surgery, my mother came to stay with me to help with the day-to-day stuff around my house. She cooked, cleaned, and drove me to appointments. My father also came for regular visits, both to be with my mom, whom he missed at home, and me, as I prepared to go under the knife. During one of these visits Dad went to see the orthopedic with me. He always had a small notebook and a maroon Montblanc pen, and he took notes on what I needed to do and what I could expect, and all the stuff that only partially sunk in as I sat in the very white examination room trying to be brave or to at least not look nervous.

When my father asked what I would not—what were the chances for success?—the orthopedic told him that he would do his best, but certain things were for God to decide. He did say he thought I would be out of pain, and that I would probably get around OK, but there had been a lot of damage. Much was unknown until after the operation. My orthopedic said that many patients could do much more after surgery than before, and in spite of all the hope that had quietly slipped away over the years, I felt like maybe things would get better. I suppose maybe I had to feel this way, so that I didn't feel like a thirty-six-year-old getting a surgery usually meant for a senior citizen. And so I could believe it was, in fact, the best choice.

At this point, perhaps you're thinking, yes, the happy ending is coming. This might make you sigh with relief, or become disenchanted with the story, feeling the happy ending wasn't earned. There's some judgment at the prospect of happiness, just like this entire story opens me up for scrutiny. Even though the surgery would help with the pain I had in my right knee, even though it partially restored what had been destroyed, it did not, of course, cure my RA. I never thought it would, and you shouldn't think that, either. I can still have swelling, fatigue, fever, aches, joint damage—any of RA's affects—at any time. I can also get around in a fairly normal way.

Happy is a relative state.

The night after my surgery I got very little sleep because I had intense pain. The night nurse had already threatened to catheterize me if I didn't urinate, and so I willed myself to pee, only to be left for forever atop a full bedpan. So things didn't start off so great that evening, and once the meds wore off, I felt like my thigh muscle was being slowly shredded with a cheese grater. That first night, my dad stood vigil by my bedside, getting only sporadic sleep in an easy chair also in my room. Luckily I didn't have to share a room with another patient. He tried desperately to get the nurse to give me something for the pain, and perhaps she did, but I honestly can't remember. I remember him holding my hand so maybe I wouldn't feel so alone, and I remember squeezing because it hurt that bad.

Dancers build muscle memory from the day-in, day-out study of technique. Over the years, my thigh muscle had learned a new muscle memory, trying to pull my kneecap up from my deteriorating joint. My orthopedic surgeon told me that even under full anesthesia my thigh muscle would not relax, still trying to manipulate the kneecap to avoid painful grinding in the joint. The body's ability to adapt to protect itself is quite remarkable in this way. My orthopedic did tell me I was the only patient in which this had happened after going under. Although he finally did get it to relax, my muscles retained a dancer's knowledge. What could have been a minor curiosity signified to me a small connection to my former self.

After the first night, things did get better, but it was slow going. My leg was strapped into a machine that helped stimulate the new joint by continually keeping it in motion as if pedaling or walking. I could lie down as this happened, or sit up propped on pillows, and many times I'd get calls from friends as the machine churned my leg, which was a welcome distraction. I learned exercises I would have to perform daily and made arrangements for physical therapy. When I was released from the hospital, I was given strong pain pills, but within only a few days, I refused to take them because I wasn't hurting so much, not comparatively, and I was worried about being dependent on them. Pain, by then, was one thing I knew how to contend with.

The weeks immediately following my surgery, I still needed the walker. My wound needed to heal, and I had to learn to walk again. I'd limped for so long, accommodating a joint that continued to fall apart, that my legs literally needed retraining on just how to correctly put one foot in front of the other.

Dance had taught me how to train, however, and so even though it took three physical therapists, and some unconventional approaches, like a Pilates reformer, as well as a manipulation of the joint under anesthesia, by my orthopedic surgeon, I finally made progress. First, though, a remarkable thing happened. As the wound from the surgery healed, I stopped hurting for the first time in what felt forever. I just felt nothing. It was bliss. My father said he watched my facial features loosen, too, and soften. He said that I looked younger, because I no longer carried the pain on my face. I didn't know it was so evident. Perhaps I'd never hidden my anguish at all, that it was there, on display, all the time.

I've never regained full mobility with my prosthetic knee, but I'm able to do things now I thought I might never do again. RA still lives in my being, waging its ongoing war against me. Take the good with bad, the saying goes, or is it the other way around? The ending isn't simply happy or sad. It isn't really an ending.

This past June I had the opportunity to renew my handicap placard for my car. But as the date for this renewal came and slipped by, I've yet to have my doctor sign the papers I'd need to file at the DMV. I can walk from any space in the lot to where I need to go. I can walk without the aid of a cane. I can walk at a normal pace and move with relative ease.

Once a week I slip the needle of a prefilled syringe into the fleshier parts of me, dispensing medicinal liquid under the skin to balance my whacked-out immune system. During the week, I will spend several hours in a studio, in the presence of dancers as their teacher. Twice a day, anti-inflammatories. All this give-and-take, but I've found an uneasy peace.

I've given you a version of my story, the best I can given I didn't want to tell it in the first place. I might craft it with the words I choose and pluck so carefully and shape through revision. What I accept is I've given you this tale and you will decide something about it and about me I have no control over. You will judge or feel or discount. Or, a concoction of all three. I can accept that once written, my story is no longer wholly mine. Still, I give it to you.

Today I am sick, and tomorrow I will be sick, as I will be every day until I die. I may not like it, but that's how it is. The rest of my life will always be entwined with rheumatoid arthritis. But it's my choice to also be something more, to still find those shadows of a dancer, which is to say tiny flecks of magic, within me. Or, like any other hopelessly in love, I will always be the keeper of a flame.

Sarah Wangler

Beatrice

Because she is fond of yellow,
she wants the moon.
The dorsal pits on a woman's pubic plate
indicate the number of infants she has
delivered. Picture: purple crinoline
dress her mother wore
for Aunt Charlotte's wedding.
She, for cousin Shayla's. Her white Easter
hat and hair curled blond—
but Beatrice asks her priest,
What shall I do if I am pregnant by you?
She's fifteen. She wants the moon.
He gives her wild carrot seed.
She chews the natural contraceptive,
Queen Anne's sand in her teeth.
Her bonnet edge is a fingerprint.
Because she is fond of yellow,
the curled blond edges, the girl
wants the moon. The girl wants
her priest. Beatrice wants wild
carrot seed. Wants fine metered lace.
Beatrice chews his seeds and
talks to grandmothers,
favorite grown-ups who teach
her that bears stay asleep longer
than weasels in spring, and
priests' hair splits and dries out
and goes gray, too.

Peycho Kanev

Eternal Circle

I sit by the window and watch
the cars on the highway. These
metallic angels of death hit my
irises and then disappear in the
horizon. I am too far away to
feel anything, too distant. I look
at an orange on the table. So orange,
so perfect! Like nothing else in
my life. But now it's getting darker.
The sun sinks behind the hills.
And I am thinking of some knife
to break the perfection of this orange,
but it rolls on the table with all
its orangeness and falls on the
floor, and I am too numb even
to move.

J. Gabriel Scala

On Choosing Childlessness

"Blind Date for Old Turtles Yielded Eggs, No Offspring"
—The New York Times, *October 8, 2008*

In the article, she is nameless, this Yangtze giant soft-shelled turtle
who had lived alone, the last living female of her species, undiscovered
inside the hull of a Chinese zoo. For half a century

no one questioned the childless ache that thrummed in her belly,
the way she sometimes sank into the murky water, eyes lowered, making
her solitary progress to the filthy bed below, the years of preparation:

fattening up and building nests, rising each year from the dark mud,
each year without child, searching out the full sun on her back, the frail
air where eggs could safely wait for one to come. The dreamed one,

the one imagined *almost* into being. And then scientists and doctors,
the zookeepers got involved—threading needles into her veins, exposing her
soft underbelly, injecting hormones, taking her far from home

to one who climbed on top, the weight of him pressing down on her,
the weight of emptiness and hope, the years of longing, bearing down
on her, that yielded eggs, hollowed out, cracked and brittle, that died

one by one. The scientists make plans for the two turtles to try again.
How can they know how the longing slows and stills, finally dissipating
into the air like the stench of a startled and dead bird who lay for hours

gently panting at the bottom of a windowpane before finally letting go?

James P. Austin

First Flood

On the afternoon her parents departed for the grocery store with twenty-two wadded singles, the girl sat in a rusty chair on the porch, watching the river swell until it nearly reached the top of the embankment across the street. For days, the heavy rains had rendered them all housebound, desperate for food and drink. The girl had hoped for a flood; when the radio voice, in its tinny urgency, predicted it, the girl felt in the rising waters a cleavage of the past from the present and, most importantly, the future.

Her father had promised to return with the groceries that would satisfy the hunger she had ignored. She imagined them grilling burgers in the front yard, listening as the river splashed ever closer. The next day, they would escape from their house, from their town, as it began to flood. They would be survivors, refugees in a new, strange town. Maybe, she dared to think, they would never come back here. Maybe there was someplace else they belonged.

By nightfall, she allowed that, while her parents had gone to the grocery, they had been waylaid. Perhaps they had stopped for a cold drink; she could hardly blame them. They had been without their favorite cold drinks ever since the rains began. Perhaps now they were just around the corner; the headlights of their approaching car would reveal a wide swath of the black river, fixing the crests. She would see the river lapping against the gravel road, bound to spill onto the street and make its way first into their home and then into town. They would grill out in spite of this—no, because if it!— there in the front yard, celebrating in the river's swollen face, late into the night.

☾

She fell asleep in that rusty chair as she waited. She took deep breaths of the sweet air rising off the river, feeling renewed, remade. She pictured the air carrying river smells like in a card she had received once, from a faraway aunt, upon which a breeze carried a red feather into the second-story bedroom window of a vast farmhouse. A small girl, forearms resting on the sill, smiled as the feather approached. Her aunt had signed the card, *Remember always, you are loved.* Her mother said the aunt was some sort of Jesus freak, but that didn't matter to the girl. She had loved that card until it went missing, and had loved it even more after it had gone.

Drowsy, half-sleeping in the darkness, the girl remembered a school trip to the town hall, where they kept records of all the historic floods in basement archives. Her class had spent but a moment in that cool, shuttered room, but the wardrobes of files captivated her. She slipped away from her class, returned to the room, and hid in a corner. She sat on the concrete floor with an open file, studying photographs.

The girl remembered one in particular, among all the photographs of downtrodden folks who had lost their homes, lost everything. There was one happy family. They paddled through a flooded Main Street, afloat among the rooftops. She could see the small eyes and the wide smiles, but the faces remained elusive, gauzy. Packed into the boat were a father, a mother, and two young children, a boy and a girl. The father stood in overalls at the bow, his long, thick body facing the invisible photographer, a hand raised and waving. The father understood that this was one for the history books. He knew he was lucky, as lives such as his disappear into nothing once they are lived.

Behind him sat the mother, wearing a dress and bonnet, her shoulders angled toward the bow, toward her husband. Her face, too, was turned to the camera. The girl discerned the semi circular orbs of the woman's regal cheekbones and the dainty chin that disappeared into her white dress, which was long and billowed out from ample hips. The mother was waving at the camera, too, in a way that could only be described as glad. In the back of the boat were the children, each with an oar in hand, the boy wearing a cap, the girl with her hair in pigtails falling across the front of her shoulders just so. They had ceased rowing and turned to the camera. They, too, were waving and smiling. They were each of the same order of happiness.

The girl, hearing her teacher calling her name in the distance, focused on the photograph with renewed vigor; she allowed herself to become drawn into the world of the photograph. The faces of the family gained color, their features sharpened, until the girl recognized the faces of her own family. The photograph was no longer an artifact. It foretold the future. Her father was leaner than in real life, stood taller. His face was square and intractable.

Her mother, meanwhile, prudently protected her face from the noonday sun with a bonnet that cast in shadow her ruddy cheeks and broad mouth, her squeezed nose. This happy face bore little resemblance to her actual mother: the bleary, defeated visage of late mornings, the soaring crimson cheeks at midnight—the girl knew it—and yet, as in dreams, she recognized this unfamiliar face as belonging to her own mother.

In back was her brother. She had imagined him many times, wondering what form a brother might take. Always he was a friend. His face was small, his features modest and sharp, his eyes dark and narrow and mischievous, eyes that had lured his sister into troublesome adventures many times. Even in the frozen scene before her, the girl could see that familiar glint in the half-closed eyes of her younger brother, as if, in the next moment, he might plunge into the muddy river water and swim the length of Main Street, inviting her to come along on another adventure that would worry their mother, until their father placed his thick arms around her shoulders and assured her, again, that their children would be fine, that they were of solid constitution and sound judgment, that they would never die.

The girl watched herself closest of all, hungry for clues to the future. She was smiling, smiling because she was happy, proud of herself and her family. The bones of the face were not hidden underneath the pasty, puffed skin of early adolescence, not like her present face. The cheekbones were affixed just beneath her eyes like pulled blinds; her jaw was lean and defined, lengthening the face, creating prominence. Their color was high. This face foretold a beauty that she would someday inherit.

Everybody was happy. This family had survived a flood. Look at them, she thought. They are liberated.

☾

186

Even before she opened her eyes in the morning, the girl knew she was alone. She was sleeping on the porch, facing away from the river. For a moment, she wondered how she had gotten there. Then she recalled moving in the blurry darkness, her body supine, the slap of water against a firm surface, a smell damp and primordial, and the concrete, cold against her cheek.

The girl had hoped to hear the scuttling sounds of breakfast, the breaking of eggs against a metal bowl, their urgent scrambling with a whisk, the sizzle of bacon on a skillet. She had hoped for yeasty muffins blooming in the oven, simmering sausage gravy, the hushed chatter around a breakfast table. This would make up for the night before, when her parents had arrived too late and seen their daughter asleep on the porch, too late to grill out—how about breakfast, just the way you like it? How about a family, presiding over its own resurrection?

But the house was silent.

When had she seen them last?

Her mother had almost departed without a word, but she paused at the porch steps. "Move those books, will you," she said after a moment.

The girl blinked and opened her mouth. "Books?" she finally said.

Her mother pointed. The girl looked down. It was true—her school books were right where she had left them. She had meant to go to school, but the swelling river had transfixed her. She had forgotten all about the books. Now that she remembered them, she thought about the happy family from the flood archives. She understood that when her family was gone, they would not be recorded in books like the ones she read for school. Nobody would know about them. They would not matter. The known past held no place for her and her family. The known past was their enemy.

She sensed her mother, arms crossed and resting on her stomach, chest sunken. The girl imagined that her mother was wondering what her daughter was *doing* staring out at the river. The girl threw back her shoulders and drew in a slow breath. She narrowed her eyes until she could only see the river, framed top and bottom by the backs of her eyelids.

The girl imagined sitting on the top step of the porch with her mother, who leaned toward her even as they both looked out to the river. The girl was speaking, but she did not know what she was saying—not the words themselves. She was speaking eloquently, pointing to the river. She was explaining to her mother, with a precision she had never known, what the river meant to her—what it meant to their family, how a catastrophe can invalidate the past, destroy history, open new ground for building.

The girl wished she had the words. She wished her mother wanted to know. But her mother would not ask, and the girl would not tell her what she had been thinking all day—for her, there would be no more late nights alone in the darkened house, her parents gone, for hours or days. No more truancy: she would be a good girl now. She would grow up to become a professor, a speaker of wisdom. The neighbors would not whisper on their porches, over cigarettes and bourbon, about her parents, who had disappeared into the lockup for vagrancy or public menace. She hated those neighbors, despised their judgment, their rickety, sidelong faces. She wanted to watch as their houses floated away in the flood. She wanted those neighbors to scream for help, help us please little girl, as she watched them float, then lurch, then drown.

Her mother unfolded her arms and came closer, looming until the girl thought the time was right to look up. This close, the girl noticed the creases on her mother's forehead and the brown spots on her cheeks. Her eyes were tiny and dark, and their hard gaze held the girl's face.

The girl looked right back.

Many times the girl had been in her room, or lying on the couch, listening to her parents arguing in the kitchen. This is where they enjoyed cold drinks, and this is where they did battle. These battles were fierce. Nothing was too much. They said horrible things the girl could not remember. They punched. They came after one another with knives. Sometimes they hit each other, or her father threw her mother across the kitchen. Eventually, the yelling and the hitting culminated in a tense, exhausted stalemate, into whimpering apologies, promises of a new path. Both were skilled intimidators; the girl had been the object of this, when she was at fault for some wrong—the cracked foundation of their home, the empty cupboards, her father's missing whiskey mug.

"I wish you'd go to school," her mother finally said, "and get the hell out of my hair."

The girl, relieved, looked away. She felt serene. Her mother could no longer find an outlet in anger. She nodded at her mother in full confidence of coming events, dipping her head until her chin nearly touched her chest. Her mother waited a moment, her eyes smaller and smaller, before she hurried off.

When her father arrived later that afternoon, the girl was still in the chair on the porch, trying to watch the river overtake some shrubbery, staring at a single bush for so long she eventually lost the ability to see it. He seemed to come from nowhere.

He wasn't a bad man. She understood that he wasn't a good man, either, whatever that meant to the people of the town. Whatever "good" was, he wasn't it, and, by association, neither was she. Her father was known as a drinker, a real drinker, a man who could out-drink everybody in town, and, after he had done that, he could drive to the next town and out-drink everybody there, too. She heard her teachers whisper it to each other as she sat quietly at her desk, writing careful letters with a steady hand.

But when he wanted to, like now, her father could straighten out his body, throw back his shoulders, and in this posture carry his considerable weight with grace, as if every last ounce belonged. She was glad to see him cut this figure, for this was the man of the future. He looked down at her, grinning. He wore his red ball cap, his favorite, stained with dry sweat and formed to the specific contours of his head. Like always, he wore it askew. He was unshaven, the hairs crawling down his neck and disappearing beneath his T-shirt.

"Mother says you're hungry," he said.

"That's not true," the girl said.

Her father sat down on the front steps and patted the concrete. She was beside him in an instant. She loved him like this. She loved the thoughtful expression on his face as he considered words. He would ask her questions and patiently listen to her answers. He treated her almost like an adult, half-friend and half-daughter, leaning in close to share some confidence, his breath clean against her cheek, *Hey, take it easy on your mother, alright kiddo? She'd never tell you this, but she loves you and wants you to do better than her; she just doesn't know she thinks it. But I know her, OK? I know that woman if I know anything. Let's keep this between us, you and me.* Even though he might speak slowly, he was not slow. The girl knew it. At his best, his manner was drawn-out and languid, like a summer afternoon. She felt the ease in his body.

He enjoyed the sound of his own voice, the atmosphere it created, that cocoon of trust containing just the two of them. She trusted him and loved him above all else in the world, and she knew he felt the same way.

He put his arm around her shoulder. "Didn't go to school, huh?" he asked, nodding soberly as if she had already answered.

The girl felt the weight of her father's massive forearm on her shoulders. "Yeah."

"Your mother and me, we never finished school," her father said. "You know that."

She nodded that she did.

"I know that you like going to school," he said. "That's right," he went on. "I know we've had to drag you back to bed sometimes when you're too sick for school. That's how bad you wanted to go. Remember?"

"Yes."

"But here you are, a nice day, and it got the better of you," her father said. "Isn't that right?"

"That's right."

Her father removed his arm; the girl's shoulders felt weak without his weight to support. "That's not it," he said, again slowly. "That's not it at all."

"It's the river," she blurted, surprising herself.

She wanted to tell her father what she meant, but also she didn't. When she looked over at him, he was looking at the river, too, appraising it with eyes of experience. They looked tremulous, those eyes, ponderous and almost, for an instant, despondent. He reached into his breast pocket and plucked out a cigarette, then lit it, all in one fluid motion. The lighter disappeared into his palm as he closed his hand.

"A flood is quite a thing," her father said, exhaling the sweet smoke. "Have I ever told you about the flood when I was a kid?"

The girl shook her head.

"Well," he said, "I won't ruin it for you. This is your first flood, and that's important for a kid who grows up on the river. It's like nothing else. Let's just say it's a very big thing."

The girl smiled and faced the river again. He was right, of course, not to tell her about the flood. She decided not to say anything, either.

They sat together silently for a time, which made the girl happy. She watched as the sun descended, its reflection lengthening on the river's surface.

Finally, her father sighed and turned to her. "But you are hungry, I'll bet," he said. He had another cigarette in his hand, which, the girl noticed, trembled only slightly. "Come on, it's OK." He looked at her directly, nudged her with his fist.

"Maybe," she said. "Maybe a little bit."

"Little bit peckish, huh," her father said, standing and turning his back to the river. As he stood, he set his cigarette, still burning, on the edge of the top step. He held his hands in fists before his chest. "How about this," he said again, clasping his hands together in a loud clap, rubbing his palms. "Tomorrow, we may have to leave the house for a few days, until this river lets up. But we're safe for tonight. Take it from me. Let's round up a few dollars, and your mother and I will go to the store for burgers and soda pop, and let's have a good time tonight, us three."

The girl stood, giving her father a hug around his waist. She felt him tense, then slowly relax and accept. His hands touched her shoulders, those rough hands, shakier than before. She hugged him harder, as if he might float away if she let him go.

"Say now," he said, "would you get Daddy's cigarette for him?" She reached down and, keeping one hand on his waist, picked up the cigarette between thumb and forefinger. "There we go," he said, backing away and lowering onto one knee, taking the cigarette in his hand. "Does that all sound like fun?"

She nodded quickly, the ends of her hair dancing on her shoulders. He turned his head and looked in the general direction of the sun. "Good," he said. He smiled, right at her face, then assumed a serious expression, one reserved, she was meant to understand, for adults. "Your mother and I will need your help."

He had been out of work, that was true, but he had one final check. Problem was, with all the banks in town closed for fear of the flood, he couldn't cash that check. Here he paused—"You know what checks are, right?"—and when she nodded, he grinned proudly at his grown-up girl, and continued. When the flood went away, the banks would reopen and he could get his cash. Until that happened, he and her mother were strapped. That's why there weren't any groceries in the house, he explained. That's why they were all hungry.

"Your mother and I feel real bad," her father said, turning to look at the river.

The girl looked, too. The sun was not far from the river now. She had been told at school not to stare at the sun, for doing so would burn its shadow onto everything she ever looked at again. She had liked the idea of that. She wanted to see the sun move in the sky. She wanted to see it always.

Her father dug his hands into his front pockets. She noticed the worn square in his back pocket, where he usually kept his wallet.

"How much?" she asked.

Her father's face brightened at her offer, as she had hoped, as she had known. He gave her a number and tousled her hair. Wordlessly, she ran up the steps, through the front door, and into her room. She lifted the corner of her mattress where she kept her money, a wad of singles she had collected here and there. Twenty-two dollars. She had kept the money for a reason, though she was never certain of the reason until that moment, when it hit her flush in the face.

She presented the bills to her father, straightening them one at a time. He watched with wide eyes as she piled one bill on top of another. He balled them in his fist and jammed them into his front pocket, smiling. "Be right back," he said pleasantly, musically, and went into the kitchen to draw up the grocery list.

He reappeared on the porch moments later, still standing tall, his shoulders arched back so far it seemed painful. He moved almost nervously. His hands were busy. He came toward her. He patted her head.

"All right, pipsqueak," he said. "I'm headed out now to meet your mother. You be good."

"OK."

"Guard the house for us. OK?"

The girl nodded, smiled. He smiled back.

"Rain's coming again," he said, dipping his chin to the west. A low bank of gray clouds hung there. She hadn't even noticed, but she welcomed the sight. The rain would come and spill the river over its banks once and for all. The next day they would paddle in a rowboat high above the submerged streets. Maybe there would be talk between her parents. Maybe she would get that brother.

After her parents left for the grocery, the girl walked alongside the embankment, which the river had finally reached. The sun had lowered into the clouds.

The rain came overnight. She remembered hearing it, the pattering of water into water.

The question had nagged throughout the night. When were they coming?

She opened her eyes to face the river. She found it had submerged their yard. It had climbed two steps up the porch. She recognized in that instant the true nature of flood water: fast and urgent, choppy and dirty, malignant. Massive pieces of driftwood bobbed past in the current. They struggled to stay afloat, turning end-over-end, sweeping from her view and disappearing for good. Balls of wet fur—skunks or dogs or possums, she couldn't tell—bobbed briefly into view before disappearing. She saw hunks of wood, bushes, a smattering of cans, a tire, a shattered rowboat. She saw the exposed roots of a tree reaching to the sky as if seeking purchase in a low cloud. She understood that this tree had been torn from the earth by the floodwaters, just as the floodwater had claimed the balls of wet fur, the driftwood.

She thought she saw a person, facing downward and relaxed, as if enjoying a dip.

The girl was on her feet. She looked around for another living person, but the other porches were deserted. Some of the old chairs and couches on those porches were now gone. She pictured the entire street, taken by the river, the current ravaging and the driftwood battering, the homes destroyed.

She was hungry now, so hungry. She thought about dying hungry and decided that it wouldn't do. If nothing else, she would die with a full belly. She could fill herself with a deep gulp of river water. She thought it was terrible that she found this idea soothing.

She went inside, hoping, somehow, that her parents had simply gone to bed and let her alone, that they were rising for coffee, shaking away the cobwebs, making prudent arrangements. She noted, again, the grimy linoleum floors in the kitchen. It had been her job to keep grime out of the small ridges in the floor, and in that she had failed, time and again. All she'd had to do was wait for her parents to give in to whatever always seemed to nag and pull them back, and the chore list, the grocery list, the things she was supposed to do to keep this house together, all became afterthoughts.

Now she remembered her father's deliberations, late at night after an argument, leaning over a mug of whiskey, surveying the soiled floor, *We ask for one little thing, a little thing, these floors spotless, and it's too much. It's too much to scrub these floors clean. What are we going to do with her?* She had failed them one too many times; she had stood in silent, burning judgment of them for too long. Her judgment, his anger, returned to her now. She was going to carry it with her into those flood waters, a sodden weight that would pull her beneath the roiling surface, where a toppling tree trunk waited to gash her face.

She continued into the living room. The clock on the wall had stopped at 11:21 a few months ago. It had been her job to change the batteries, and for an instant, she was seized by the need to finally do that.

Instead, she hurried into her bedroom in the back of the house, and stood wondering if her mattress could become a raft. She pressed her hand against the heavy fabric she had long considered her sanctuary when things were bad. It would kill her. It would sink, she knew.

The basement would be safe, she decided. There were no windows down there. She threw open the basement door and started down. She stopped when she smelled musty dampness. She retreated when she heard water smacking against the concrete, the flood waters hunting her even from beneath.

The girl returned to the top of the steps and rested her chin in her palms. She listened to the water in the basement, lapping insistently toward her. She heard the river outside, sloshing eagerly.

In her panic, the girl resolved to make a list, of all the things she would do, once the flood waters had spared her. She would scrub that linoleum, hands and knees, every week. She would keep her father's whiskey mug pristine and always where he wanted it. She would change the batteries in the clock. She would send a message to her parents, to the world, that she had learned her terrible lesson but good.

She headed for the kitchen to draw up her list, walking with military precision, warding off death by enumerating her many wrongs: *did not scrub floor, did not keep whiskey mug clean, did not understand mother and father enough, did not sleep when told to sleep, did not stop crying when told to stop crying, did not stop giving dirty looks when they said mean things to me.* That was a start, she decided, not nearly enough but a start, something she could keep to herself, a tally of wrongs redressed.

The grocery list her father had written was in the first drawer she opened, among the pens and scratch paper she sought. She picked it up, held it close to her face. Her father had written three things: *burgers, buns, soda pop.* The words were ridged and uneven, each character a painful toil.

All thoughts of composing her own futile list disappeared. She placed the grocery list back in the drawer. She looked out the front door and saw that the river was even with the porch now. She walked into her bedroom and dragged her desk into the living room, then went back for her blanket. She pushed everything off the desk and spread the blanket on top. She was very tired. She lay on the desk surface, closed her eyes, felt at peace with fatigue. She couldn't understand now how she had ever felt anything but fatigue.

When she heard distant voices and oars moving water, she opened her eyes and sat up on her desk. The clouds had broken, the sun was shining.

She returned to the porch. The heat had returned. The river had receded, enough to reveal the porch steps. It was still vast, and massive objects still bobbed in the water, but the current had slowed, the surface of the water smooth but for the wake of a half dozen rowboats out scavenging. Someone waved at her, asking after her safety. She called back that she was fine, just fine. Catastrophe had not occurred, after all. The past had not been cleaved away.

She felt relief at that. She wondered if her desperate bargaining had found a sympathetic listener. No, she thought, remembering her father's grocery list. She wanted to see that list again. She read it at the same table where her father had composed it. She stared hard at the labored handwriting. She ran her fingers sideways over the deep-pressed ridges of the characters. This was, she knew, her first love letter.

Reviews

Wild Girls by Mary Stuart Atwell. New York: Simon & Schuster, 2012. 271 pages. $25, cloth.

In her debut novel, Mary Stuart Atwell tells the story of a town infamous for turning girls wild, and of Kate, the girl determined to escape the town and its mysterious curse.

Swan River rests at the foot of the Appalachian Mountains, but despite its boasts of a prestigious private school and charming local culture, the town is anything but peaceful. The girls of Swan River take girl power to a literal level, as they glow, fly through the air, and set buildings and cars on fire with just a touch of their fingers.

Atwell does an excellent job of capturing two complicated portraits: that of a girl torn between a prim private school existence and a dysfunctional family life, and that of her tumultuous, enigmatic hometown.

Atwell takes elements from Kate's adolescence and draws out the hidden gravity of each piece as Kate becomes intertwined with the curse of the wild girls. The novel starts with Kate on a commune farm playing pranks on boys; four years later, the same setting becomes the scene of a tragic fire blazing with family secrets. Throughout the novel, Atwell uses this technique to uncover the complexities of Swan River as Kate is developing into an adult, since Kate's growing wisdom provides her with insight to the mysteries of the town. Atwell is able to suspend the reader's belief as the form of the novel follows the content from the ordinary to the extraordinary. The novel transforms from a coming-of-age story to a dark mystery composed of fantastical elements, while managing to hold on to the bones of both genres.

Atwell weaves together the lives of Swan River's women, highlighting the common threads as well as the unique facets of women in different perspectives, from the richest prep school girls to the poor girls on the commune. Kate and her sister Maggie attend a party where the local women are throwing empty bottles of wine against the wall of the Tastee-Freez. When the sheriff tries to intercede, the women aim the bottles towards his car and he speeds off. Young Kate is astonished by the depravity of the women, but as Maggie explains, "Of course they're pissed off. [...] Half the girls I knew in middle school are divorced, Kate. They've got little kids, the men are all morons or assholes, and they can't make a living. Everything's going out of business. Most of the houses in the Delta are for sale."

Atwell blends the youthful experiences of friendships and first loves with themes of poverty and repression to add depth to this fantastical coming-of-age novel. Meanwhile, the reader wonders whether Kate will go wild and whether this town of Deadheads and private school debutantes will go up in flames at the hand of the wild girls. In a town like Swan River, who could blame a girl for going a little wild?

—Jessica Boykin, *Moon City Review*

☾

In the House Upon the Dirt Between the Lake and the Woods by Matt Bell. New York: Soho Press, Inc. 2013. 320 pages. $25.95, cloth.

Matt Bell's debut novel *In the House Upon the Dirt Between the Lake and the Woods* immerses readers in a haunting allegory of marriage, parenthood, and loss, winding a mythical labyrinth of sentient creatures and buried memory.

Bell presents the story of a newlywed couple who move away from civilization to lead a simple life sustained by the land, only to find they are unable to rear a healthy baby. The husband, and narrator of this tale, becomes estranged by his wife's inability to produce a healthy child and is thereafter haunted by the voice of his first miscarried son. When his wife mysteriously disappears into the woods and returns with a boy, the husband denies his role in the child's creation and denounces his family, causing his wife to sing into creation and inhabit a new home far below the surface of the earth. Readers are greeted to the novel with the husband's foreboding warning:

> How terrible we must have seemed that day, when together we were made to believe our marriage would then and always be celebrated, by ceremony and by feasting, by the right applause of a hundred kith and kin. And then later how we were terrible again, upon this far lonelier shore, where when we came we came alone.

Isolation and indecision permeate the husband's journey to retrieve his wife from the depths of the earth as he fights the subversive voice of his miscarried firstborn telling him to abandon the thought of starting anew. In a particularly memorable scene, the husband sorts through rooms of distant memory sung into existence by his wife. In these rooms, he encounters first love letters he and his wife wrote to each other, the first time they made love, the promise he made to keep her safe, and the unraveling of these promises in arguments. Readers are left with a haunting image of the narrator explaining how he touched his wife, "How every time it left a mark."

The remarkable achievement of *In the House Upon the Dirt Between the Lake and the Woods* is the meticulously crafted and always-haunting prose that often waxes poetic and the way it submerges readers in uncertainty with the narrator. Although clarity can be elusive at times, Bell's creation of stark images and use of repetition conjures a fabulist world full of characters, voices, and images that stick around long after the pages run out. A fierce and wise bear that rules the woods, an old and sentient squid, a giant butterfly occupying an isolated room of memory: these are the images to decipher and cherish. *In the House Upon the Dirt Between the Lake and the* Woods is a novel in which to revel. Its readers won't soon forget Bell's unforgiving yet compassionate journey into the nature of family, memory, and loss.

—Joseph Lucido, *Moon City Review*

☾

Rise: Stories by L. Annette Binder. Louisville, Kentucky: Sarabande Books, 2012. $15.95, paper.

Picking up a short story collection from a new author can be a risky proposition. In the case of *Rise*, that risk is rewarded in surprising and heartfelt ways. The collection begins with a story that exists on the outskirts of reality, and it never stops toeing that line. L. Annette Binder's prose has the ability to make a reader question what is truth within its pages in the best possible way. The question of what is and what isn't remains unanswered throughout the collection, and that is how it should be.

If there is a connection between the short stories, it is in the themes of identity and religion. Binder's characters are often questioning their surroundings in a way that could be deemed existential, and their questions have a way of permeating beyond the characters and into the reader's mind. As the characters question their identity, or even when they refuse to question it, they become empathically portrayed archetypes of insecurity in our society. The misunderstood other, the mother of an ill child, the man who accidentally killed someone, and the invalid are all given a sound depiction that rings true in the feeling, even if the details border on the fantastic.

As with any collection, there are a few standout stories. In the best stories of the collection, it feels like something mythological is at play within the pages, as in the story "Dead Languages." This story follows a couple whose son has a strange ability: "His arms went tight sometimes when the words came. His eyes rolled back in his head. All those words, all those musical sounds. Their boy said them with conviction, and none of them made sense." While this story could become simply about the fact that the child speaks in languages that there is no way he could know, it focuses more on the mother's ability to cope with the strange occurrence. This is done without any heavy-handed push in any direction (even as the child is speaking in tongues), and it feels like a hopeless situation is unfolding. Stories like this one leave the reader wanting more.

Rise is a collection that is best consumed in small pieces, and there is plenty of intellectual nourishment to be had within. The sheer variety of the stories is enough to provide something for any reader that might want to pick up the collection. It is a testament to Binder's ability as a writer that she makes such diverse characters come to life. The world portrayed here is "strange and familiar both," and that is a real treat to see.

—Matt Kimberlin, *Moon City Review*

☾

A Land More Kind Than Home by Wiley Cash. New York: William Morrow, 2012. 320 pages. $24.99, cloth.

It is no simple task to capture the closed-off inner sanctum of rural Appalachian existence. The subject matter demands painstaking attention to detail, as the characters in such a story have likely always lived in such a setting, as did their parents before them. The characters know their surroundings intimately. The names of towns, roads, plants, families—little is a mystery. The author must take this into account. Wiley Cash, brings all the knowledge gleaned from growing up in North Carolina to *A Land More Kind Than Home*, and the book bristles with life for his expertise. The novel, dense but not bogged down with detail, delivers gut punches with subtely, all the while immersing the reader in a world Cash appears to know all too well.

The story itself nearly collapses under the weight of those details, and as the tragedy unfolds, the author paints himself into a corner wherein he is forced to drudge up backstory just as the narrative is gaining steam. This shift in storytelling is noticeable, but not devastating. Cash collects his prose and reestablishes his characters, thus regaining his footing quickly.

Those well-formed characters provide the lifeblood of Cash's novel, with three major players serving as first-person narrators. The novel shifts perspective every few chapters, telling the story in a languid Southern dialect quite befitting to the subject matter. These three characters—the son, the sheriff, and the midwife—weave between the three of them a story of death, religion, betrayal, and demise. The supporting cast is equally well handled. The alcoholic grandfather, cheating church lady, and hypocrite minister could all easily drop into caricature. However, Cash breathes true life into every character, and the novel works because of his attention to detail.

Cash's prose is delicate, yet confident. His style blends the colloquial with the literary, and this works well for him, for the most part.

There are moments when readers may find themselves questioning the likelihood that characters who often confuse their verb tenses and proper pronoun usage would actually have certain words in the vocabulary. These instances are few and far between, though, and do not detract overall from the story.

A Land More Kind Than Home succeeds far more often than it does not. Cash's first novel presents a compelling human story, replete with tension that builds like the slow roll of a summer rain threatening to crest the very mountains that provide the book's backdrop. Much like many small towns that don't much care for strangers asking questions, this story will haunt any reader inquisitive enough to go snooping for answers.

—Derek Cowsert, Moon City Review

☾

Red Army Red: Poems by Jehanne Dubrow. Evanston, Illinois: TriQuarterly Books/Northwestern University Press, 2012. 73 pages. $16.95, paper.

The power of the State and of the body are concepts woven throughout Jehanne Dubrow's fourth collection, *Red Army Red*. The cover image—perfect rows of bullets, graced front and center by a tube of red lipstick—symbolizes sexuality in the midst of severity, the book's central theme, and we witness this juxtaposition through the eyes of a young girl coming of age behind the Iron Curtain.

"Chernobyl Year," the first poem, establishes the metaphors of awakening sexuality and a changing government, with the profundity of the personal and the historical intersecting:

> We were uneasy in our skins,
> sixth grade, a year for blowing up,
> for learning that nothing contains
>
> that heat which comes from growing[.]

Most of the opening section, "cold war," observes people maneuvering the Communist landscape. We see the sexuality of prostitutes who "wore their hair red army red" and the struggle to toe the government line while simply remaining healthy:

> and 1 + 1 would always equal red
> and red the baby's name first word first step

> the scarlet fever when the pills ran out
> the mouth that swallowed every cure for red.

"Bribes My Family Made" is a pantoum about what can be traded, most of which is sex. The first line, "for seven pairs of jeans you get a maid," galvanizes that truth when it reappears, slightly altered, as the last line: "for seven maids you get a pair of jeans."

Poems turn toward a personal body politic in "velvet revolution," the second section. "Five-Year Plan" begins, "Like the Soviets, my body had a plan / for every phase of development." In the poem "Velvet Revolution," the speaker confesses

> there was a mutiny
> called sex, a violence like
> the riot that she'd seen

> on the nightly news.

Change is predestined and necessary, though the passage may be traumatic.

The final section, "laissez-faire," takes us past the fall of Communism and into the forced embrace of laissez-faire economics. Here, puberty becomes *Wall Street*'s Gordon Gekko; deprivation becomes excess. Nevertheless, current experiences exist against the backdrop of our own histories.

Dubrow, the daughter of American diplomats, spent a portion of her youth in Communist-era Poland, and that perspective is prevalent as *Red Army Red* takes us through the pains of governmental and personal revolution, the lure and power of sexuality, and how, even when starved for food or affection, the body will have its way.

—Sara Burge, Missouri State University

☾

Leaving Tulsa by Jennifer Elise Foerster. Tucscon, Arizona: University of Arizona Press, 2013. 89 pages. $15.95, paper.

Leaving Tulsa, the full-length collection of poetry by Jennifer Elise Foerster, brings the reader along on an at once immediate and ancient journey through the American West in four parts. Foerster, a member of the Muscogee (Creek) Nation of Oklahoma, spins image-heavy tales of a gritty, distinctly Midwestern brand of melancholy that focus on displacement and loss, but also on harvesting the vestiges of a vanishing culture. The reader is allowed a window through which to view the speaker's interactions with a dying grandmother and with land steeped richly in family and cultural history, becoming skeletal over time in the dust of Oklahoma summers, as well as with a journey West dotted with mystery and loss.

Leaving Tulsa is a collection of poems that act as relics themselves of a specific life and a particular past, but Foerster calls on the reader to participate in cataloguing what might have been lost with stunning imagery that blooms from the overgrown fields—though she still reminds us of the ugliness of desolation and carelessness of progress. In "Leaving Tulsa," Foerster writes,

> Grandma fell in love with a truck driver,
> grew watermelons by the pond
> on our Indian allotment,
> took us fishing for dragonflies.
> When the bulldozers came
> with their documents from the city
> and a truckload of pipelines,
> her shotgun was already loaded.

As the journey through *Leaving Tulsa* advances, Foerster explores the juxtaposition of death and what survives, of feeling "othered" while at the same time being born of the silt and the soil. Foerster creates a flow of language that becomes more consuming as the road stretches before the reader, and images of ribs and bone cages—of something unspeakable and elemental existing between the land and the body—deepen the reader's connection to Foerster's intense and lyrical visions.

Attention to land and loss is carried out through the very end. *Leaving Tulsa*'s fourth and final section, "Vanishing Point," finds the speaker trekking across the desert of the American West, simultaneously departing the spilled remnants of a resonant past and bringing traces along for the journey. The reader encounters characters and interactions that while, always striking, don't always fully reveal themselves, leaving the speaker's migration suffused in the language of loss and carefully guided mystery.

Foerster's *Leaving Tulsa* is a collection of striking images of wear and deterioration and the language of rebuilding. In "Going West," Foerster writes, "How fertile the earth / because of our death." The poems, though at times press us to identify our own referents in the disparate narrative, and are small monuments to a past found in the minerals of the earth. The collection guides the reader in the role of silent observer as Foerster chronicles the human experience against a timeless American backdrop.

— Satarah Wheeler, Moon City Review

☾

Notes for a Praise Book by Jeff Hardin. Durham, North Carolina: Jacar Press, 2012. 53 pages. $13.95, paper.

Jeff Hardin's poetry offers a glimpse of Tennessee landscapes, crops begging for harvest, and dim backwoods trails that most of us should not venture down. But it's not important where Jeff Hardin was born, or where he now resides. Whether intentional or not, *Notes for a Praise Book*, Hardin's latest collection, is more of an understanding of how one's surroundings can produce something unique from our mundane lives, rather than the importance of where our feet land.

"What's the gist of the gist," he asks in "Ellipses for the Rain on Its Way," rendering any kind of summary useless. Poets often bury secrets from their readers, but Hardin seems eager to share the secrets of his bean rows and yard plums, while still managing to maintain an air of mystery. One of the standout poems in this collection, "Agreements," challenges the beauty of a Claude Monet painting, with Hardin offering up childhood images of hard-wrought gardens as something to be studied and enjoyed, then and now. There is no hostility in his challenge, just the belief that his dusty world is also a work of art, that the plain fields we overlook can move us, if we only allow it.

Often we rely on rah-rah spirits to keep the cracks from showing whenever a crisis appears, especially in rural areas where everything seems so far away. But Hardin isn't trying to hide the familiar; rather, he embraces what we already know, and uses the scenery and people of "Notes" to show that familiarity doesn't always mean ordinary.

Hardin's world is one where hard work pays off. "Notes" is about sometimes wanting to lie down and give up, but instead polishing the rough edges with a smile and realizing just how lucky we might be. His work moves back and forth through family generations with all the speed of thistle seed caught in the wind, and we know that he is carrying these lessons with him from person to person. Sometimes the generations are blurry, and we can only guess if Hardin is reliving a moment from his childhood or watching his own children experience it. Regardless, Hardin isn't wasteful. "Imagine no one ever saying an excess word," he writes in "From a Day of Falling Snow." We get the feeling Hardin believes that he's not alone in imagining this, a world where we weigh each word and thought with caution, all the while keeping an appreciative eye on what's growing around us.

—Anthony Isaac Bradley, *Moon City Review*

☾

Easy Math by Lauren Shapiro. Louisville, Kentucky: Sarabande Books, 2013. 65 pages. $14.95, paper.

In "They Promised Me a Thousand Years of Peace," Lauren Shapiro writes, "The way I feel about mathematics bespeaks a love / of theory in which the proposition never / leads to the conclusion." The enjoyment I felt reading *Easy Math* sounds similar. Shapiro sets up a series of propositions—"A hundred stuffed animals / and I can't make the claw catch," "the ghost of Bambi's mother arrives," or "pixilated hamburgers … how many times they will be eaten / in virtual restaurants around the world"—but although each poem ends succinctly, they resist conclusion. Shapiro refuses to sum up the images she presents; indeed, she seems instead to relish the randomness of the world around us.

Hers is a world of improbable juxtapositions: "a hopeful sun / rising over aisle fifteen," African warlords and guinea pigs, Isaac Newton plus pineapple suckers, astronauts that watch *Dateline*. Despite the collages *Easy Math* presents, however, don't think Shapiro rambles or assembles without care. She is a sharp-eyed observer, and her details and words are carefully chosen. The poems are concise, moving crisply from line to line, achieving endings that are never obvious and always precise.

Shapiro questions constantly throughout her work. "Would I be a genius if I really got it? If the math equation / became the never-ending movie of my life," she asks in "The Life of Birds." In the poem "The Encounter," Clara Barton and Florence Nightingale meet to ask the questions we all ask: "Do you believe in God?" Does everything happen for a reason?" "Are you married?" and "Would you like to come over for dinner?"

In my favorite poem of the collection, "Please Support the Wisconsin Guinea Pig Rescue League," Shapiro writes, "I am committed to disrupting complacency. I have carried / my microscope out of the lab and into every American's home." Listen to how she begins "Canis Soupus":

> On their way to the East Coast, the West Coast coyotes
> mated with wolves and dogs. They didn't do it
> to improve their species. Who thinks like that?

The answer, of course, is that humans do. Shapiro's microscope is turned unwaveringly on us. The poem's last two lines read, "We've engineered all breeds of dogs as candidates / for Best in Show. Now what's to show?" Indeed, "What kind of crazy world is this?" the poems in *Easy Math* all seem to ask. In Shapiro's book, the answers add up to surprise and delight. Her world is our world – inscrutable, the mundane made strange, and above all comic, the kind of math in which the sum is more than the total of its parts.

—Lora Knight, *Moon City Review*

☾

Huang Po and the Dimensions of Love by Wally Swist. Carbondale, Illinois: Southern Illinois University Press. 2012. 96 pages. $15.95, paper.

Huang Po and the Dimensions of Love's cover features white clouds swimming in an ocean of blue sky. In the foreground, a stone horse rears onto its hind legs, as if wishing to charge vertically, bursting through the clouds above. This juxtaposition of imagery serves as a great symbol of the poetry crafted by Wally Swist.

Throughout his twentieth collection of poetry (including his chapbook publications), Swist uses the couplet with the finesse of a fencer wielding a rapier and dagger. Each line expresses sound, rhythm, and emotion which bring the reader into Swist's world, hiking alongside him; yet, the partnering line balances the reader, parrying their progression, slowing the pace, forcing one to truly examine the scenery Swist presents.

While Swist earns his reputation for excellent pastoral poetry with the opening poem, "October," wherein Swist writes,

> an owl hoots and hoots; my breath steams the air,
> and the first hard frost spreads its silver crystals
> through the boreal forest, then begins
> to shine through the moonlight in October.

In addition to creating a precise scene of nature imagery this also serves as a prime example of Swist's control of language. More importantly, his use of sound to layer his poetry into a multidimensional state, showcases Swist's mastery of alliteration and assonance.

Throughout his collection the sound and in some cases the visual concept of poems combine with the natural elements being described to pull the reader deeper into the landscape, such as with "Roaring Brook" where Swist writes of

> The sounds of the water
>   falling down the mountain
>   sliding from consonance
>
> to assonance so many times
>   they entwine to become the spool
>   of a spoken word, voice itself, fluidity.

As prime example of Swist's synesthetic approach, the reader first notices the placement of each line, forming a crude waterfall. Then the poem's action in combination with the sounds of the words themselves creates an effect that is purely that of water.

Another interesting aspect is that despite being in awe of the natural world, Swist never seems to narrow his respect to focusing upon one source of religion as inspiration for nature's beauty. He instead moves from Christianity with "The Annunciation," a description of the painting by Botticelli, into reflections of a Zen master with the book's titular poem, "Huang Po and the Dimensions of Love," before moving further west, and to yet another religious aspect from history, with his poem "To Psyche."

In addition to moving through the spiritual from various sources, Swist's collection begins with the poem "October," and as the work progresses, Swist accompanies his reader through each turn of the seasons, beginning with the fall, moving through winter, spring, and summer, and ending with the speaker preparing for yet another cold snap, because everything is cyclical, after all.

—Timothy Leyrson, *Moon City Review*

Contributors' Notes

Jeffrey Alfier has work forthcoming in *Poetry Ireland Review*, *South Carolina Review*, and *Tulane Review*. His latest chapbook is *The City Without Her* (Kindred Spirit Press, 2012), and his first full-length book of poems, *The Wolf Yearling*, is forthcoming from Pecan Grove Press.

James P. Austin earned his Master of Fine Arts degree from the University of California, Irvine, and has attended residencies in Ireland and the United States. His fiction has appeared previously in *Mid-American Review*.

Jessica Boykin is a fiction writer and an instructor at Missouri State University. She recently received her Master of Arts in English from MSU.

Lori Brack's poems have recently appeared in *Mid-American Review*, *Superstition Review*, and *The Prose-Poem Project*, and in the anthologies *Begin Again* (Woodley Press, 2011) and *To the Stars Through Difficulties* (Mammoth Publications, 2012). Her chapbook, *A Fine Place to See the Sky*, is a poetic script for performance art by Ernesto Pujol and was published in 2010 by the Field School, New York.

Anthony Isaac Bradley's stories and poems have appeared or are forthcoming in *Slipstream*, *Penduline Press*, *SLAB*, *Main Street Rag*, *Weave Magazine*, *Elder Mountain*, and *The MacGuffin*.

Sara Burge's first book, *Apocalypse Ranch*, won the De Novo Award and was published by C&R Press in 2010. Her poems have appeared in *The Virginia Quarterly Review*, *River Styx*, *Cimarron Review*, *Court Green*, *The Los Angeles Review*, and elsewhere.

Sarah Carson was born and raised in Flint, Michigan, and now lives in Chicago. She is also the author of three chapbooks, *Before Onstar*

(Etched Press, 2010), *Twenty-Two* (Finishing Line Press, 2011), and *When You Leave* (H_NGM_N, 2012). She blogs at sarahamycarson. wordpress.com.

Matt Cashion is the author of a novel *How the Sun Shines on Noise* (Livingston Press, 2004). Other work has appeared in *Willow Springs, The Sun, Northwest Review, Fugue, Passages North*, and elsewhere. He teaches creative writing and literature at the University of Wisconsin-La Crosse.

Grant Clauser is the author of the book *The Trouble With Rivers* (FootHills Publishing, 2012). Poems have appeared in *The Literary Review, Painted Bride Quarterly, Cortland Review, Sow's Ear Poetry Review*, and other journals.

Derek Cowsert is currently finishing his MA in English from Missouri State University. Upon graduation, he plans to pursue an MFA in fiction.

Heather Cox founded and edits *Ghost Ocean Magazine* and Tree Light Books. Her work has appeared or is forthcoming in *Mid-American Review, PANK, Toad Suck Review, Columbia Poetry Review*, and *Midwestern Gothic*, among other journals.

Cherie Hunter Day's prose poems and microfictions have been published in *Mid-American Review, Mississippi Review, Quick Fiction*, and *Wigleaf.* She lives in Cupertino, California.

Trista Edwards is a PhD student at the University of North Texas, where she is currently working on her degree in poetry. Her work has been published in *32 Poems, Mid-American Review, The Journal, iO: A Journal of New American Poetry*, and other journals. She lives in Denton, Texas.

Jacek M. Frączak is a visual artist, designer, and assistant professor in the Art and Design Department at Missouri State University. He was born in Warsaw, Poland, and moved to Springfield in 2007. He has had thirty solo shows in Poland, Denmark, Germany, and the United States, and his etchings, drawings and photos are featured in many European museums, as well as in Springfield and in private collections.

Ryan Gannon teaches English, edits nonfiction for *OJO*, and studies fiction at Wichita State University's MFA program. His work has appeared in the online journals *Knee-Jerk* and *Staccato*.

D. Gilson holds an MFA from Chatham University and is currently a PhD student in American Literature & Culture at George Washington University. His chapbook, *Catch & Release*, won the 2011 Robin Becker Chapbook Prize from Seven Kitchens Press.

Charity Gingerich completed her MFA at West Virginia University, where she is currently teaching poetry and composition. Her work has appeared in *Ruminate Magazine*, *Center for Mennonite Writing Journal*, *Connotation Press*, *Poetry South*, and *Dappled Things*.

Kelly Goss recently graduated with an MA from Miami University. She currently lives in Ann Arbor, Michigan, where she's working on a story collection and teaching at Washtenaw Community College. This is her first publication.

Jeff Gundy's sixth book of poems, *Somewhere Near Defiance*, will be published by Anhinga in 2014. His book on theopoetics, *Songs from an Empty Cage: Poetry, Mystery, Anabaptism, and Peace*, is forthcoming from Cascadia. He teaches at Bluffton University in Ohio.

Becky Hagenston's first story collection, *A Gram of Mars*, won the Mary McCarthy Prize and was published by Sarabande Books in 1998; her second collection, *Strange Weather*, won the Spokane Prize and was published by Press 53 in 2010. She is an associate professor of English at Mississippi State University.

W. Todd Kaneko lives and writes in Grand Rapids, Michigan, and teaches at Grand Valley State University. His work has appeared in *Bellingham Review*, *The Los Angeles Review*, *Southeast Review*, *NANO Fiction*, *The Collagist*, and elsewhere.

Peycho Kanev is the editor-in-chief of Kanev Books. His poetry collection, *Bone Silence*, was released in September 2010 by Desperanto. A new collection of his poetry, *Requiem for One Night*, will be published by SixteenFourteen in 2013.

Matt Kimberlin is a graduate student in English at Missouri State University. He is currently serving as an assistant editor for *Moon City Review*.

Lora Knight is currently working on a MA in English at Missouri State University. Her poems have appeared in *Elder Mountain* and *Cave Region Review*.

Gerry LaFemina is celebrating 2013 with the publication of a new collection of prose poems, *Notes from the Novice Ventriloquist* (Mayapple Press), and his first novel, *Clamor* (Cordorus Press). He's the author of nine other books of poetry and prose and directs the Frostburg Center for Creative Writing at Frostburg State University, where he is an associate professor of English.

Gary Leising is the author of a chapbook of poems, *Fastened to a Dying Animal*, published by Pudding House Press in 2010. His work has appeared or is forthcoming in *River Styx*, *The Cincinnati Review*, *Prairie Schooner*, *Sentence: A Journal of Prose Poetics*, and *Mid-American Review*.

Michael Levan received his MFA from Western Michigan University and PhD from the University of Tennessee. Currently he is an instructor of writing at California University of Pennsylvania. His work can be found in recent or forthcoming issues of *American Literary Review*, *Natural Bridge*, *Mid-American Review*, *New South*, and *Fifth Wednesday*.

Alexis Levitin's translations from the Portuguese and Spanish have appeared in well over two hundred literary magazines, including *Kenyon Review*, *American Poetry Review*, *New Letters*, *Mid-American Review*, *New England Review*, and *Prairie Schooner*. His thirty-two books of translations include *Blood of the Sun* by the Brazilian poet Salgado Maranhao (Milkweed Editions, 2012).

Timothy Leyrson's poetry has appeared in *Midwestern Gothic* and *Atticus Review Online*. He pursuing his MA in English from Missouri State University.

Joseph Lucido is a graduate student studying fiction writing at Missouri State University.

Conor Robin Madigan's first novel, *Cut Up* (2012), is available from The Republic of Letters Books. His work is also forthcoming in *Ginosko Literary Journal.*

Rick Marlatt is the author of two award-winning chapbooks of poetry; *How We Fall Apart* was chosen as the winner of the 2010 Seven Circle Press Poetry Award, and *Desired Altitude* was named the winner of the 2012 Standing Rock Cultural Arts Prize.

Neil Mathison's essays and short stories have appeared in *The Ontario Review, The Georgia Review, Southern Humanities Review, North American Review, Agni, Pangolin Papers, Blue Mesa Review,* and elsewhere.

Melanie McCabe is a high school English and creative writing teacher in Arlington, Virginia. Her first book, *History of the Body,* was published by David Robert Books in 2012. Her work has appeared on *Poetry Daily,* as well as in *Best New Poets 2010, The Georgia Review, The Cincinnati Review, Bellingham Review, Alaska Quarterly Review, Shenandoah,* and many other journals.

Joe Meno is a fiction writer and playwright who lives in Chicago. He is the winner of the Nelson Algren Literary Award, a Pushcart Prize, and the Great Lakes Book Award, and a finalist for the Story Prize. He is the author of six novels, including the bestsellers *Hairstyles of the Damned* (Akashic Books, 2004) and *The Boy Detective Fails* (Akashic Books, 2006). He is an associate professor in the Fiction Writing Department at Columbia College.

Travis Mossotti was awarded the 2011 May Swenson Poetry Award by contest judge Garrison Keillor for his first collection of poems, *About the Dead* (Utah State University Press, 2011), and his chapbook, *My Life as an Island,* was published with Moon City Press in 2013.

Jed Myers' poems have appeared in *Prairie Schooner, Nimrod International Journal, Golden Atlanta Review, Quiddity, Fugue,* and elsewhere. He's a psychiatrist with his own practice and teaches at the University of Washington.

Renée K. Nicholson lives in Morgantown, West Virginia, splitting her pursuits between dance and writing. She has earned teaching certification through the American Ballet Theatre and an MFA in writing from West Virginia University, where shes serves as assistant director of the West Virginia Writers' Workshop. Her writing has appeared in *Perigee: A Journal of the Arts, Paste, Poets & Writers, The Superstition Review, The Gettysburg Review,* and elsewhere.

Joey R. Poole lives in Florence, South Carolina, with his wife and infant son. His fiction and nonfiction appear in journals such as *The Southeast Review, Adirondack Review,* and *Tampa Review Online,* and the upcoming anthology *The Man Date: 15 Bromance Stories.*

R. Elena Prieto is a graduate of the Southern Illinois University MFA program. Her work has appeared in *Compass Rose, The Rondeau Roundup, A Face to Meet the Faces: An Anthology of Contemporary Persona Poetry,* and *Off the Coast.*

J. Gabriel Scala's work has appeared or is forthcoming in such journals as *Creative Nonfiction, Quarter After Eight,* and *Sierra Nevada Review,* among others. Her chapbook, *Twenty Questions for Robbie Dunkle,* was awarded the Wick Poetry Prize in 2004.

David Shumate is the author of three books of prose poetry, *High Water Mark* (2004), *The Floating Bridge* (2008), and *Kimonos in the Closet* (forthcoming, fall 2013), all published by the University of Pittsburgh Press. His poetry has also been anthologized in *The Best American Poetry* and *Good Poems for Hard Times.* He lives in Zionsville, Indiana, and teaches at Marian University.

Erin Elizabeth Smith is the author of *The Fear of Being Found* (Three Candles Press, 2008) and *The Naming of Strays* (Gold Wake Press, 2011). Her poems have appeared in numerous journals, including *Mid-American Review, 32 Poems, Zone 3, Gargoyle, Cimarron Review,* and *Crab Orchard Review.*

J. David Stevens teaches creative writing at the University of Richmond. His most recent stories appear or are forthcoming in *The Southern Review, Gulf Coast, Mid-American Review*, and *NANO Fiction.*

Chris L. Terry's first novel, *Zero Fade*, is being published September by Curbside Splendor. He has an MFA from Columbia College Chicago and works teaching juvenile inmates.

Lindsay Tigue writes poetry and fiction and her work has been published or is forthcoming in *Indiana Review, Cutbank, Drunken Boat, Barnstorm*, and *LIT*. She won the 2012 Indiana Review 1/2 K Prize and currently studies in the MFA program at Iowa State University.

Carmen Vascones has published five collections of poetry, including her collected poetry in *Oasis de voces* (*Oasis of Voices*) (Casa de la Cultura, Quito, 2011). Her work has appeared in anthologies and magazines published in Canada, Puerto Rico, Mexico, Colombia, Chile, Peru, Brazil, France, Spain, Germany, and Italy. In the United States, she has appeared in *Per Contra, Bitter Oleander, Birmingham Poetry Review*, and *Hampden-Sydney Poetry Review.*

Benjamin Vogt is the author of a poetry collection, *Afterimage* (Stephen F. Austin State University Press, 2013), and has a PhD from the University of Nebraska. His poetry and nonfiction have recently appeared in *Crab Orchard Review, DIAGRAM, Orion, Sou'wester, Subtropics*, and *The Sun*. He blogs at *The Deep Middle.*

Court Walsh was a public school teacher before she retired and took to writing fiction. Her stories have appeared in *Hunger Mountain, The New Orphic Review, The Long Story, Callaloo*, and *Uncle John's Bathroom Reader.*

Sarah Wangler's poems have appeared in the *Best New Poets* anthology, *Cream City Review, FIELD, Superstition Review, The Tusculum Review*, and previously in *Moon City Review*. She currently serves as an associate editor for the *Southern Indiana Review.*

Gabriel Welsch is the author of four collections of poems, the most recent of which are *The Four Horsepersons of a Disappointing Apocalypse* (Steel Toe Books, 2013) and *The Death of Flying Things* (WordTech Editions, 2012). Recent fiction appears in *The Southern Review*, *New Letters*, *CutBank*, *New Madrid Journal*, and *PANK*.

Satarah Wheeler is a graduate student at Missouri State University. Her poetry has appeared in journals such as *Midwestern Gothic* and *Elder Mountain*.

Sarah Williams' current body of work focuses on her roots in the rural Midwest. She is an assistant professor of painting and drawing at Missouri State University.

Mark Wisniewski's novels are *Show Up, Look Good* (Gival Press, 2011) and *Confessions of a Polish Used Car Salesman* (Hi Jinx Press, 1997). Fiction of his has appeared in *Virginia Quarterly Review*, *Antioch Review*, *New England Review*, *The Southern Review*, *The Missouri Review*, and *The Georgia Review*. He has won a Pushcart Prize, and his work has appeared in *Best American Short Stories*.

Francine Witte's flash fiction chapbook, *The Wind Twirls Everything*, was published by MuscleHead Press in 2011. She is the winner of the Thomas A. Wilhelmus Award in fiction from Ropewalk Press, and her chapbook, *Cold June*, was published in 2010. Her poetry chapbook, *First Rain*, was published in 2009 by Pecan Grove Press.

AGNI

TESTING THE EDGE

SINCE 1972

WWW.AGNIMAGAZINE.ORG
CODE PN06 FOR 20%
NEW SUBSCRIPTONS

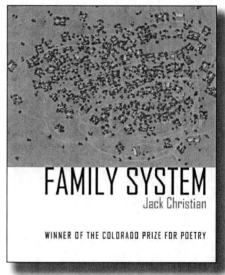

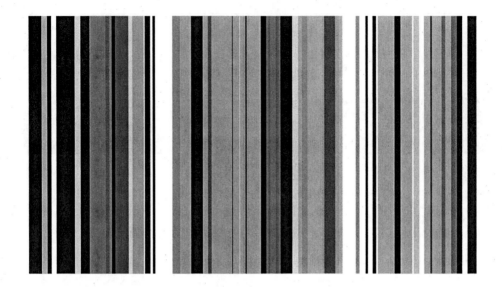

MID-AMERICAN REVIEW's

Fineline ²⁰¹³ *Competition*

for Prose Poems, Shorts Shorts, & Anything In Between

$1000 First Prize

2013 Final Judge: Richard Garcia

Full info: www.bgsu.edu/midamericanreview

Fiction Poetry Essays
Reviews Interviews Art

Carolyne Wright   Brian Turner   Albert Goldbarth
Marilyn Hacker   Clancy Martin   Alice Friman
Robin Hemley   Mia Leonin   Stephen Dunn
Daniel Woodrell   Hilary Masters   Mark Irwin
Andrea Hollander Budy   Gary Soto   Donald Hall
Linda Pastan   Ray Young Bear   Mary Jo Bang

New Letters

www.newletters.org

University House/University of Missouri-Kansas City
5101 Rockhill Road, Kansas City, Missouri 64110
(816) 235-1168

Photos, sculpture, and banana-fiber doll design by Gloria Baker Feinstein.
Art photo by E. G. Shempf. From New Letters vol. 76 no. 3.

THE
SAINT ANN'S
REVIEW

Viola Moriarty

www.saintannsreview.com

Moon City Press

2013 BLUE MOON POETRY CHAPBOOK CONTEST

Complete Guidelines
mooncitypress.com/chapbook/

Submissions
mooncitypress.submittable.com/submit

Deadline
April 15, 2013

CPSIA information can be obtained
at www.ICGtesting.com
Printed in the USA
FFOW04n2046100114

9 780913 785447